Get Started

Teach® Yourself

Get Started in Franchising

Kurt Illetschko

For UK order enquiries: please contact Bookpoint Ltd,
130 Milton Park, Abingdon, Oxon OX14 4SB.
Telephone: +44 (0) 1235 827720. Fax: +44 (0) 1235 400454.
Lines are open 09.00–17.00, Monday to Saturday, with a 24-hour
message answering service. Details about our titles and how to order
are available at www.teachyourself.co.uk

Long renowned as the authoritative source for self-guided learning –
with more than 50 million copies sold worldwide – the **Teach Yourself**
series includes over 500 titles in the fields of languages, crafts,
hobbies, business, computing and education.

British Library Cataloguing in Publication Data:
a catalogue record for this title is available from the British Library.

ISBN 978 1444 100297

This edition published 2010.

Previously published as *Teach Yourself Franchising*

The **Teach Yourself** name is a registered trade mark of Hodder
Headline.

Copyright © 2006, 2010 Kurt Illetschko

Typeset by MPS Limited, A Macmillan Company.

Printed in Great Britain for Hodder Education, an Hachette UK
Company, 338 Euston Road, London, NW1 3BH, by
CPI Cox & Wyman, Reading, Berkshire RG1 8EX.

The publisher has used its best endeavours to ensure that the URLs
for external websites referred to in this book are correct and active at
the time of going to press. However, the publisher and the author have
no responsibility for the websites and can make no guarantee that a
site will remain live or that the content will remain relevant, decent or
appropriate.

Hachette's policy is to use papers that are natural, renewable and
recyclable products and made from wood grown in sustainable forests.
The logging and manufacturing processes are expected to conform to
the environmental regulations of the country of origin.

Impression number   10 9 8 7 6 5 4 3 2 1

Year   2014 2013 2012 2011 2010

Acknowledgements

This book is the result of almost 40 years of exposure to franchising. In course of my work, I have interviewed hundreds of franchisors, franchisees and franchise practitioners from various parts of the world. I am indebted to them all, but will not try your patience by listing them individually. However, contributions by a few individuals stand out.

First, there is my long-suffering life partner, Anita. Without her, I could not have done it; only someone who lives with a writer who is passionate about his work and works from home can understand the trials and tribulations she has to endure.

Then there is my friend and mentor Eric Parker, a franchise expert *par excellence* who is living proof that franchising is an international concept. After helping to set up a food franchise in South Africa, he went on to take the concept into several countries located on three continents where the brand continues to notch up successes against ferocious international competition. His love for franchising serves as an inspiration to me when the going gets tough.

While I was writing the first edition of this book, Doug Wilkie, a Glasgow-based franchise expert, did lots of legwork for me and also reviewed the final draft of this book. The miracles of electronic communications notwithstanding, some issues are best resolved through personal intervention and I remain indebted to Doug for doing just that. I must also thank Greg Nathan for permission to include some of his groundbreaking work on the Franchisee Lifecycle Concept, named by him the E factor, which has evolved into an international standard on this topic.

Lastly, I must thank Alison Frecknall of Hodder Education for her guidance, encouragement and patience. Many thanks to you all for helping me to turn this into an authoritative read.

Kurt

Credits

Front cover: Copyright © Dino O

Contents

Meet the author

**I became acquainted with franchising back in 1975 when
I made an investment in a quick-printing franchise.** Although
franchising was well established in the USA by then, the
concept was in its infancy in other countries. I knew absolutely
nothing about franchising at the time, but I am a quick learner
and the more I found out about franchising the more excited
I became by its potential. I soon purchased a share in the
franchisor company, thereby graduating from franchisee
to franchisor. A few years later, I sold my business to focus
exclusively on the promotion of the concept.

**For the past 30 years, I have worked hard to advance
franchising.** During this period, I had the pleasure of observing
literally thousands of people making the transition, either
from employee to franchisee or from the owner of one modest
business to the head of a franchised network. Most of these
transitions were extremely successful but there were also
some that failed.

**Most of those who experienced the bitter taste of failure
blamed franchising for their misfortune.** While this is
perfectly understandable, it is neither constructive nor fair. In
my experience, even the most rudimentary investigation of any
so-called franchise failure reveals a different picture. Rarely,
if ever, is the concept of franchising at the root of a franchise
failure but its haphazard implementation. On occasion, fraud
also comes into play but fortunately this is the exception rather
than the rule.

I remain convinced that franchising, if implemented correctly,
is the surest route to business success. However, every
business venture carries an element of risk and a franchise
is no exception. To protect yourself, you need to be informed.
This is the sole reason why I agreed to my publisher's request

to rewrite this book. My intention is to tell you how franchising works, warts and all, just like I have done in the first edition.

You could be forgiven for wondering what a guy who was born in Austria and has been residing in South Africa for almost 40 years can tell you about franchising as it is practised in other countries but this is one thing you don't need to worry about. The concept of franchising originated in the USA but has been applied successfully and without significant adaptation all around the world.

Ever since I have become a self-appointed promoter of franchising, I have travelled the world to attend workshops on the topic and generally study the application of franchising. I have come to the conclusion that no matter where in the world you find yourself, franchising is practised in the same way. And regardless of whether you plan to become a franchisee or a franchisor, you will soon find that both these roles are closely intertwined. For a network to be successful in the long term, the franchisor and its franchisees need to work together for mutual benefit.

Once you have worked through this book, you will be able to decide whether entering the exciting world of franchising is the right career move for you. I have tried to cover the topic as comprehensively as possible, and Chapter 7 contains a list of useful references for further enquiry. If, after exhausting these avenues, you are left with questions relating to any aspect of the concept, but not questions regarding specific franchise opportunities, feel free to email me. I will respond promptly and do my best to help.

Kurt H. Illetschko
franchise@intekom.co.za

Foreword

Whichfranchise.com are pleased to write a few words of introduction to *Get Started in Franchising*, welcoming the opportunity of getting our message out to anyone with an interest in the fascinating subject of franchising.

We have been involved in helping people explore the option of franchising for over 20 years. We have witnessed life changing stories both good and bad and are aware of so many hard working franchise owners earning money way beyond their original expectations.

For those of you who are considering franchising as a way into starting your own business, we urge you to do so with great care as no business venture is without risk. You must be 100% sure the challenges of running your own business are for you; if so, buying a franchise is the right way into owning your own business. Franchising is not for everyone. If you are convinced franchising is for you then you must do your research very carefully to ensure the franchise you chose matches your skills experience and aspiration.

In addition to this book there is much help out there ranging from specialist seminars to banks with specialist franchise departments who really understand franchising to quality legal advice from franchise solicitors. Your National Franchise Association will have details of the best advisors in each field.

The Whichfranchise.com team
http://www.whichfranchise.com/

Only got a minute?

Those unfortunate souls who lost their jobs during the most recent downturn in the economy are living proof that the term 'employment for life' has become a myth. Of course, the economy moves in cycles and the current downturn will pass but who knows when the next upturn will peter out, to be followed by another downturn, and another ... There is yet another thing to consider. Even during periods when the economy is strong, mergers, acquisitions and other corporate strategies will be followed by rationalization drives and jobs will be lost.

Should you consider starting your own business but balk at the perceived risks, ask yourself this question. Given the uncertainties of the world economy, what could be riskier than depending on others to keep you employed? Of course, there are risks attached to starting your own business. The free enterprise system can be a harsh task master but this does not mean that you have to fail. You just have to be extra careful.

After assessing your strengths and weaknesses realistically, you need to take some calculated risks. Going the franchise route fits precisely into this scenario. The slogan 'being in business for yourself but not by yourself' sums up what it is all about. Investing in a franchise allows you to enter entrepreneurship with a safety net. And no, it doesn't mean that you have to flip burgers for the rest of your life, unless of course you choose to. Opportunities in franchising are no longer limited to quick service restaurants. Check out some of the websites we list in Chapter 7 of this book and you will see what I mean.

Which brings me to the final hurdle many would-be entrepreneurs encounter: capital or, to be more precise, lack thereof. Because most franchises are highly formalized, investment levels are relatively high. This is not necessarily a bad thing because customers are more likely to trust a business that is properly resourced. This tends to result in the payback period being shorter than if you run a makeshift operation. There is also a marked willingness among commercial banks to offer franchisees of reputable franchisors preferential access to loans.

5 Only got five minutes?

Many people are dreaming of starting their own businesses some day in the future but for whatever reason, it remains exactly that: a dream. Some try to justify their reluctance to move into entrepreneurship by referring to the attendant risks. Especially if they have a family, they reason that it would be irresponsible of them to risk all by following their dream. Others claim that the right opportunity had not come along and it makes more sense for them to stay in their current job until it does.

This kind of reasoning may have had some validity in the past when job security was the order of the day but it has now lost its validity. Recent developments in the world economy left many unemployed and the prognosis for the future isn't much better. Yes, the economy will recover and companies will start hiring again but even during economic boom times, corporate mergers, downsizing and other management techniques will see to it that the lot of an employee will remain tenuous at best. Do you really want to contend with these uncertainties for the rest of your working life?

Just consider this: among the dangers that lurk in this brave new world we live in is the unpalatable fact that to stay competitive, companies either took over other companies or were themselves taken over. This means that a corporate manager who may located in another part of the world has the power to move a business from one country to another, be it in pursuit of cheaper labour, attractive tax breaks or both. This can happen regardless of how qualified and hardworking this employee may be.

Now is the time to make your move

Now for the good news: Experience has taught us that every downturn is followed by an upturn. The current period of economic gloom and doom is no exception to this rule. While it is true that certain 'holy cows', for example the notion of employment for life, have become outdated, new opportunities have evolved. You can exploit them by starting a business of your own. Now, someone may have told you that starting a small business is a risky proposition at the best of times; doing so during a downturn in the economy would be sheer lunacy. I disagree with this assertion and I will tell you why.

While it would be foolish of me to deny that starting a business contains an element of risk, it is equally true that if you are the right person, select the venture with care, ensure adequate funding and practise a high level of work ethic, success is unlikely to elude you. And starting a business during an economic downturn offers many advantages to the shrewd investor. Property owners are more inclined to offer attractive rentals, suppliers will cut prices to secure your business and the labour market is awash with skilled individuals who have lost their jobs through no fault of their own.

Best of all, there is absolutely no need for you to face the unknown by yourself. Franchising has been with us for over five decades. Far from being based on hype, franchising has evolved into the most successful business expansion mechanism the world has ever known.

The way I see it, franchising's success secret is deceptively simple: an entrepreneur develops a comprehensive business concept and hones it to perfection. When the business is ready for a national roll-out, its owners decide to do so by franchising it. This accelerates the process because franchisees invest their own money and are motivated to succeed.

What makes franchising attractive?

Seen from the viewpoint of an established entrepreneur, franchising is attractive because prospective franchisees invest not only their own money but also inject passion and hard work into the new branch. This is in sharp contrast to expansion through branches where the entrepreneur is forced to fund the expansion and has to rely on salaried managers to operate the business.

Seen from the franchisee's viewpoint, franchising is attractive because he or she is the owner of the business and entitled to keep all the profits it generates. Moreover, the franchisor will train the franchisee in the best way of operating the business and grant him or her the right to trade under the common trademark.

Franchising offers a host of advantages but in my view, its real magic lies in the interdependence between the role players. I maintain that as long as the franchise is structured correctly, the franchisor will not profit from the relationship to any significant extent unless the franchisees in the network are successful. It is easy to see that this will motivate the franchisor to support its franchisees to the hilt.

Financial arrangements

The fees that are typically charged in a franchise can be divided into initial fee (or upfront fee) and an ongoing fee, usually described as a management services fee. Most franchised networks also collect a fee that is used to collectively fund the cost of product marketing. In addition, it is the franchisee's responsibility to fund the setting up of the business and provide the necessary working capital.

The **initial fee** is a fixed amount that is almost akin to a joining fee. It is usually payable at the time when the franchise agreement is signed and pays for assistance with site selection, the establishment of the business, initial training for franchisee and staff and, in suitable circumstances, access to preferential sources of supply. The actual amount varies greatly, not so much from one network to the other but from one industry sector to another. The reason for this is that the time and effort it takes the franchisor to set up one franchisee in business is affected by the complexity of operating the business.

The **management services fee** pays for the cost of ongoing support and allows the franchisor to make a profit. In most instances, it is calculated as a percentage of the franchisee's sales and is payable in arrears, usually within a week or so after the end of the reporting month.

Some franchisors levy a fixed monthly fee but most bona fide franchise practitioners frown upon this practice. It removes the joint risk-taking aspect which should be at the heart of every franchise arrangement. A short-sighted franchisor could recruit large numbers of franchisees then sit back and collect fee income from them without providing any worthwhile assistance in return. In the long term, such an approach would not be sustainable and the network would surely fail but this self-styled franchisor would still walk away with a sizeable sum of money.

Management services can range from 1 per cent to 8 per cent or more. In industry sectors where sales are high but margins relatively low, for example in certain retail operations, 1 per cent may be all the franchisee can afford. Volume ensures that the arrangement remains attractive for the franchisor. Higher percentages are common in industry sectors where gross margins are high but sales levels relatively low, for example in plumbing repairs.

I would advise you not to become bogged down by the percentage figure of franchise fees charged. In my view, this is irrelevant. What counts is what the franchisee can expect to receive in exchange for the ongoing payments. Raising this point in discussions with established franchisees in the network will provide valuable insights.

The **marketing fee** is sometimes referred to as a contribution to the advertising fund. In most instances, it is calculated in the same way as the management services fee but legitimate exceptions exist.

To increase its ability to fund major campaigns and plan them well in advance, a network may decide to levy a fixed monthly fee. As long is this money is spent on product advertising and all franchisees in the network benefit equally, this practice is acceptable.

Some networks charge **other fees**, usually in exchange for providing services that go beyond the normal obligations of the franchisor and are therefore not covered by the management services fee. An example is an administration fee charged in exchange for providing a centralized administration service to franchisees. This may offer franchisees genuine benefits, especially if most of the franchised businesses are relatively small and the employment of an administrative assistant would not be justified. Care must be taken to ensure that such practices do not erode the franchisee's profitability.

Legal implications of franchising

In a bona fide franchise arrangement, the agreement between the franchisor and the franchisee is recorded in a franchise agreement. This is a substantial document that should set out the rights and obligations of both parties. Unlike many other commercial agreements, franchise agreements need to take the interests of both parties into account. This notwithstanding, the franchise agreement will be weighted in favour of the franchisor. This is necessary because the franchisor must have the power to enforce uniformity in the widest sense of the word throughout the network.

Franchise agreements are usually not negotiable. There are at least two valid reasons for this:

1   *The success of the network depends on a trust relationship plus enthusiastic co-operation between the franchisor and all franchisees. If one franchisee were to discover that another franchisee was granted more favourable terms, this trust may be destroyed.*

2 *Mature networks can have hundreds of franchisees. If each one of them were given a customized franchise agreement, administration of the network would be an absolute nightmare.*

The franchise agreement is a long-term agreement, usually extending over five to seven years; some franchise agreements run for up to 20 years. The franchise agreement will contain a renewal clause in favour of the franchisee. When the original franchise agreement comes to an end, the franchisee will have the right to extend it by a similar period but this may be subject to certain conditions as set out in the franchise agreement.

The franchise agreement should address what will happen if the franchisee should wish to sell the business. Although the franchisee owns the business, the franchisor will wish to control who becomes a member of the network. It is customary, therefore, that the franchisor reserves the right to veto the sale of the franchise to a person that does not meet the basic admission criteria in force at the time.

The sale may also be subject to the incoming franchisee being willing to sign a franchise agreement and undergo training. Should the franchisee die and no suitable heir is willing to take over, the franchisor will usually operate the business on behalf of the estate until a new franchisee can be found.

Where to from here?

If you can locate a franchise you can be passionate about, are willing to conform to its operational guidelines and have adequate funding, going the franchise route is the safest way to take charge of your life and become your own boss. However, not all franchises are created equal and none come with a guarantee. The onus is on you to undertake an in-depth investigation. This book will show you how to obtain the information you need to make an informed decision.

10 Only got ten minutes?

Although within the small business environment, the term 'franchising' is frequently used its true meaning is not always understood. Reckless entrepreneurs continue to interpret it as it suits their specific needs and their unfortunate victims fail to notice. This is surprising because over the past five decades, franchising has built up a formidable track record. Perhaps this is the problem. When aspiring entrepreneurs come across a business opportunity that is presented to them as a franchise, they automatically assume that it is the real thing and don't bother to investigate its merits. By the time they find out that they were duped, they have lost their lives' savings.

People who made the wrong investment tend to blame franchising for their misfortune. This is understandable but it is also grossly unfair. I am convinced that a bona fide franchise is the safest access route to your own business and I will provide you with knowledge you need to differentiate between a bona fide franchise offer and its look-alikes.

What is a franchise?

Essentially a franchise is a blueprint to business success. Investing in a franchise will not guarantee your success in business but the concept should be structured in such a way that if you follow the franchisor's instructions to the letter, you should stand a better than average chance to become successful. It follows that for a concept to qualify as a franchise, it must have been operated by the founding entrepreneur for a reasonable period. One year is generally seen as the absolute minimum.

During this time, the founder should have honed the concept to perfection. Depending on the needs of the business, all aspects of market research, product development, production, distribution, installation, administration and control should have been honed to perfection. Most importantly, every step that is necessary to operate the business successfully must have been documented and the company's intellectual property must be legally protected. Until this has been done properly, no franchise exists.

Even this is only the beginning of the long thorny road the founder of a franchise needs to travel before the concept should be launched. More specifically, the founder most put the necessary infrastructure for franchisee selection, training, initial and ongoing support in place. Although this costs lots of money, it's the only way for the creation of a franchise network that will stand the test of time.

A widely accepted formal definition of 'franchising' in its modern-day usage within the small business environment reads as follows: 'A franchise is a grant by the franchisor to the franchisee, entitling the latter to the use of a complete business package containing all the elements necessary to establish a previously untrained person in the franchised business and enable him/her to operate it on an ongoing basis, according to guidelines supplied, efficiently and profitably.'

What are the responsibilities of the parties?

For a franchise to be successful, it must be a two-way street. To ensure that a franchise offer lives up to its inherent promise, its stakeholders, namely the franchisor and its franchisees, must be totally committed towards making the venture successful. The franchisor must be willing to enter into the arrangement with the intention of creating win–win outcomes while the franchisee must want to be in business for himself but not by himself.

THE FRANCHISOR'S OBLIGATIONS

I have already said that extensive testing of the concept followed by the creation of a comprehensive franchise package should precede the launch of a franchise. But while this is a good starting point, it is not enough. When rolling out the franchise, the franchisor is under a moral obligation to screen applicants with care. Unless a candidate meets all the requirements set out in the profile of the ideal franchisee the franchisor will have created, he or she needs to be rejected.

This is not only in the interest of the applicant who, if unsuited to the type of business, would almost certainly experience failure, but also in the interest of the network. Under-performing franchisees are bad for the image of the brand, and a drain on the franchisor's resources. In this context, it is necessary to remember that although an applicant's financial standing is important, the mere fact that he or she can support the necessary investment should never be the decisive factor.

For the same reason, full disclosure of all the facts to a qualified prospect needs to be aware of to make an informed decision to join the network is essential.

As soon as the franchise agreement has been signed, the franchisor must make a team of experts available that will guide the new franchisee through the pitfalls of setting up the business. Subject to industry sector requirements, this may include assistance with site selection and lease negotiations and getting the unit ready for the grand opening as quickly as possible. In this context, the franchisor has a moral obligation to ensure that the new unit is set up at the lowest possible cost without sacrificing standards.

Training of the new franchisee and, in suitable circumstances his or her staff, in all aspects of operating the business is another imperative.

The franchisor should take a hand in an appropriate opening promotion to ensure that when the franchisee opens the doors of his or her business for the first time, the target market population is aware of the new arrival. At that point, a franchisor representative should spend a few days at the new unit to ensure that everything operates smoothly.

On an ongoing basis, franchisor representatives should provide the franchisee with market information, ongoing training, joint purchasing and advertising as well as general advertising and business support. Review of the unit's financial performance, including benchmarking against similar units within the network or active in the same industry sector, followed by practical suggestions on how these figures may be improved, is another important obligation.

The arranging of periodic get-togethers where all members of the network can discuss issues of common interest with franchisor representatives, followed by appropriate action where desirable, are other essential support services.

THE FRANCHISEE'S OBLIGATIONS

While the franchisor is under a moral obligation to select franchisees with care, the onus is on you as a prospective franchisee to undertake a careful evaluation of your skills and interests. This exercise should include a realistic assessment of your ability to finance the setting-up and ongoing operation of a unit of a specific brand.

Don't fall into the trap of thinking that you want to invest in a particular sector because of its perceived profitability. It has been shown time and again that unless an entrepreneur is passionate about the business, the results he or she achieves will be mediocre at best. So, when you meet with the franchisor, be open and honest about your background and your motivation for wanting to join this particular franchise.

Instead of rushing into a franchise arrangement, you should spend an adequate amount of time investigating the pros and cons of the opportunity. This should include interviews with established franchisees within the network and working in a company-owned unit for a period to confirm affinity. Provided that you leave the rose-tinted glasses at home, this should go a long way towards preventing a bout of 'buyer's remorse'.

Upon reaching a decision to join a specific network but before signing the franchise agreement, I advise you to consult with an attorney who

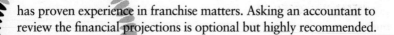

has proven experience in franchise matters. Asking an accountant to review the financial projections is optional but highly recommended.

As a franchisee you will be obliged to adhere to the network's guidelines for the establishment and operation of the business. Don't fight it, if you don't like the way the brand operates or if you are convinced that you could do better on your own, you should not have joined.

Having invested lots of your hard-earned money into the franchise, you are entitled to utilise all the support services the network offers. Since the network's franchisee support staff have done it all before, probably not just once but many times over, ask them for advice when you need it and trust their answers. On a more informal level, you will also have access to other franchisees within the network. Speak to them openly about your problems. Chances are that they have come across similar hurdles and have found a way to overcome them. That's what being a franchisee is about.

Being responsible in handling money is another requirement for maintaining a good relationship with your franchisor. It's not good enough to pay just your franchise fees on time; you need to pay your bills on time as well. Your franchisor will worry about this because poor payment performance by just one member of the network could affect the standing of the brand.

If you don't agree with one of the franchisor's decisions, take it up with the person concerned but do not broadcast it to all and sundry. By becoming a franchisee, you have become a member of a family and need to show loyalty.

What are the financial implications of becoming a franchisee?

As a franchisee, you will enter into a series of financial obligations that can be divided into initial and ongoing commitments.

INITIAL OBLIGATIONS

▶ *Upfront fee. The franchisor will expect you to pay an upfront fee. This is a fixed amount which you pay in exchange for being granted access to the network and receiving initial training and support. It does not pay for the establishment of your business and normally becomes payable when you sign the franchise agreement.*

▶ *Setting-up costs. You are responsible for the cost of setting up and equipping the business unit.*

▶ *Working capital provisions. When you start operations, you will have to pay various deposits and meet all the expenses that arise, for example salaries and shop rental. Depending on the industry sector, it may take several months or even longer before the business reaches break-even point. Once the business is up and running, you need to fund its ongoing growth. This could require increased stock holdings or your debtors book could grow. For this you need working capital.*

▶ *Personal living expenses. While sales build up, you and your family continue to have living expenses and you need to make provision for that.*

ONGOING OBLIGATIONS

▶ *Management services fee. This fee is usually calculated as a percentage of your sales and is payable monthly in arrears. The actual percentage charged varies widely from one industry sector to another, depending on trading margins and likely sales volumes. Franchisors will disclose this figure in their initial information material. When you do the financial projections for your future franchise, you need to work out whether you can afford the payment, make a reasonable return on your investment and pay yourself a market-related salary.*

▶ *Contribution to the advertising fund. Most networks levy an additional amount that is earmarked for national product advertising. This amount can either be calculated as a percentage of sales or it can be a fixed sum, payable monthly.*

▶ *Other fees. Some franchisors provide services to their franchisees that exceed the customary level of franchisee support. An example is an administration service. Any such services should offer you economies of scale.*

FUNDING A FRANCHISE

Bankers are usually well informed about franchising and are franchise-friendly for a reason. Experience has taught them that franchisees of reputable franchisors stand a significantly better chance of making the grade than wild-eyed entrepreneurs whose ideas may or may not work. Although franchisors will generally not provide funding or offer to act as surety, they will maintain contact with at least one of the leading commercial banks and facilitate an introduction. Various support schemes for prospective franchisees are in place and I deal with this in some detail in Chapter 7 of this book. This notwithstanding, you need to be prepared for the fact that funders will expect you to contribute a reasonable portion of the total funding requirements from your own resources.

What are the legal implications of becoming a franchisee?

In every proper franchise arrangement, the rights and obligations of the parties are set out in a franchise agreement. In most instances, this will be a substantial agreement, simply because it has to deal with a large range of issues ranging from the grant of the franchise to what happens if the agreement comes to an end.

In most instances, a franchise is granted for a fixed period, usually for five to ten years. Depending on the complexity of the business and the level of investment its establishment requires, the initial contract period could be as long as 20 years. The cardinal rule is that the contract period should be longer than the number of years it will take you to pay off the loan you expect to take out, plus one or two additional years so that you can reap some profits.

Furthermore, it is common practice to grant a franchisee the right to renew the contract for a further period of equal duration. The grant of the renewal is often conditional. The franchisor will want to ensure, firstly, that you have complied with all material obligations as set out in the franchise agreement. Secondly, the agreement may stipulate that its renewal is subject to you remodelling the store to ensure that it conforms to the then current image of the network. It is also customary for the franchisor to insist that when the agreement comes up for renewal, the franchisee signs a new agreement which will be identical to the agreement then offered to new franchisees.

It would be unrealistic to expect that you can negotiate a franchise agreement. Very few franchisors will agree to that, and with good reason. Firstly, the franchisor typically spends a significant amount of money in legal fees to have the franchise agreement drawn up. This fee can only be recouped by spreading it over a large number of franchise transactions. Secondly, if every franchisee in the network would have a different agreement, administration would be difficult and petty jealousies would arise because franchisees would suspect that their peers enjoy advantageous terms.

My advice is that you should study the franchise agreement carefully, have it explained by an experienced attorney then either accept it or walk away from the deal. Under no circumstances should you sign a franchise agreement if it contains clauses you are not prepared to accept. You might think that certain clauses will never be enforced but this is unrealistic. Everything that is written into the agreement is enforceable and you will have to live with it.

As a franchisee, you own the infrastructure of the business but not the brand and other intellectual property the franchisor provides. In other words, the franchisor grants you the right to operate under its brand name using its proprietary methods but this grant is subject to you operating the business in the manner set out in the network's operations manual. Should you fail to do that, the franchisor will have the right to demand performance, failing which the grant may be withdrawn.

The franchise agreement should reflect your right to sell the business but this will be subject to certain conditions that will be reflected in the franchise agreement. While some franchisors are content to reserve the right to screen incoming franchisees, others will reserve the right of first refusal. This means that if and when you want to sell the business, you will have to offer it to the franchisor first. Your offer should be based on the best price you could achieve in the open market and proof of this in the form of a credible offer to purchase may be required.

The franchisor will then have a laid down period, usually 30 days, within which it can decide to accept or reject your offer. If the franchisor is unwilling to purchase the business, you will be entitled to sell to a third party, but subject to the purchaser being acceptable to the franchisor. This will usually be determined in line with the 'ideal franchisee profile' the network uses at the time the sale takes place.

Where do I find credible franchise opportunities?

This is the easy part. Walk down any high street or visit any shopping centre and you will be surrounded by franchise opportunities. Seeing that most networks grant territorial protection, established franchisees will not see you as a potential competitor but will be quite happy to refer you to their head office.

Should you wish to invest in a franchise that does not operate from high profile premises, for example a service franchise like plumbing repairs or gutter installations, franchise exhibitions and advertisements in magazines, daily and weekly newspapers are an excellent source. And then of course there is the Internet. Several excellent sites that list bona fide franchise opportunities only exist. The best thing about them is that you can search them according to various criteria like industry sector, investment level, geographic location, etc.

You can also use the Internet to obtain details of forthcoming franchise exhibitions and other franchise-related events. If you visit one of those, the sheer number of opportunities that are on offer may overwhelm you. The best way of dealing with this is to find out in advance who the exhibitors are and compile a shortlist of opportunities that are of specific interest to you. A growing number of exhibition organisers provide this type of information on their websites, failing which you could try to obtain a copy of the exhibitor catalogue in advance.

How do I approach a franchisor?

Precisely because large numbers of franchise opportunities exist and new ones are emerging all the time, competition for good prospects is fierce. This may indicate to you that you are entering a 'buyer's market' but this is not necessarily true. While there is indeed a surfeit of opportunities, not all franchises are created equal. Those with a good track record tend to have a waiting list of qualified prospects, all eager to join their networks. This is especially the case if the success of the business is linked to certain site characteristics. If suitable sites are in short supply, the network's ability to expand is constraint.

To a certain extent, this is ameliorated by the fact that in most countries, franchising has come of age by now. As a result, a growing number of existing franchises come up for resale, often because their owners wish to retire. Investing in an established outlet can be an excellent opportunity because it adds the local goodwill the franchisee has built up, often over many years, to the brand's national appeal.

Should you come across such an opportunity, you need to be careful to make it clear early-on where your loyalties lie. The outgoing franchisee will want to negotiate a good price for the business and delay introducing you to the franchisor for as long as possible. This is not in your own best interest, however, because while the seller will be content to take your money and fade out, you will have to work with the franchisor in future. I'd advise you, therefore, to insist on making contact with a senior franchisor representative as early as possible. Because the franchisor will have to work with you in future, its representatives will be your allies. For the transaction to materialize, you need the franchisor's blessing anyway, so why delay?

Begin by drawing up a shortlist of franchise opportunities that interest you and contact the franchisors concerned. Request their franchise information kit, sit back and wait. Cross those franchisors that are slow to respond off your list immediately. If they are non-responsive at the courting stage, they are unlikely to treat you any better once you have become their franchisee.

Have at least one, preferably several, get-to-know-each-other sessions with several franchisors. As you eliminate those that no longer apply, you will eventually be left with one opportunity. If the company has a disclosure document available, study it carefully. If not, ask them for all salient details and take the trouble to work through them step by step. If everything pans out, have your legal advisor and your accountant review the opportunity then sign on the bottom line, file the franchise agreement away in a safe place and report for initial training. At this point, your new life as a franchisee has started and your future is in your hands. With dedication and willingness to work hard on your part and the assistance of your franchisor, it will be bright indeed.

1

Introduction to franchising

In this chapter you will learn:
- *how franchising developed*
- *what other options for assisted entrepreneurship exist*
- *what the advantages and disadvantages of franchising are*
- *where franchising is headed*

Franchising is widely promoted as 'a model to business success' and broadly speaking, this claim is justified. The concept's consistent growth over the past five decades is proof supreme that it can live up to its implied promise. This does not mean, however, that every business venture labelled a franchise is automatically successful. Franchising has the capacity to ease new entrepreneurs into the world of business but ultimately their success depends on several factors:

▶ *The franchise must be built on solid foundations*
▶ *The quality of the business model must be beyond reproach*
▶ *The network's support infrastructure must be fully developed and diligently applied*
▶ *The franchisee must be willing and able to follow the franchisor's business model.*

By ignoring these pre-conditions for success in franchising, opponents of the concept create the impression that investing in a franchise is not as safe as it is made out to be; this is hardly fair. This is the same as if someone would blame a precision tool used by an incompetent workman for the shoddy article this workman produces.

I am not saying that franchises never fail. Failures do occur, some in a spectacular fashion. But if you analyse the reasons for such failures, you will soon discover that the most rudimentary principles of sound franchising were ignored. On occasion, fraud also comes into play but fortunately, incidents of outright fraud are the exception rather than the rule. I also believe that the fraudsters' chances of success would be non-existent if only their victims would do their homework properly.

The information contained in this chapter will help you to understand how a proper franchise concept works. To provide you with a balanced picture, I will also describe the workings of several other business models that are sometimes presented as franchises but are nothing of the sort. Armed with this knowledge, you will be in a much better position to decide, firstly, whether franchising is the best route for you to take and secondly, whether the opportunity that attracts you is real or make-believe.

The development of franchising

Evidence exists that a rudimentary form of franchising was first used in China around 200 BC. Throughout the Middle Ages, several subsequent attempts to operate franchises were recorded but they failed to stand the test of time. It was only during the 1860s that the US-based Singer Sewing Machine Corporation developed an enduring franchise model. Not only did this step help Singer attain market dominance in their market sector and maintain it for a very long time, it also secured them a place in the history of franchising.

THE PRODUCT FRANCHISE MODEL

Singer established a network of franchised dealers who were licensed to sell and service sewing machines. The franchise format developed by Singer was to become known as a product franchise. Before long, it was applied in several industry sectors, notably in the distribution of motorcars, petrol and soft drinks. But although product franchising continues to have its followers to this day, it does have some serious shortcomings. This has prompted an irreversible decrease in its popularity, with business format franchising increasingly taking its place. Its superiority is such that most established product franchises are gradually being converted to business format franchises. This requires mutual consent in most cases, proof supreme that franchisors and their franchisees recognize the benefits a business format franchise offers.

THE BUSINESS FORMAT FRANCHISE MODEL

A business format franchise is a refinement of the product franchise model. Essential differences between a product franchise and a business format franchise revolve around two issues:

1 *The level of initial and ongoing support a franchisee can expect to receive.*
2 *The extent of control over operations the franchisor is entitled to exercise.*

In a typical product franchise arrangement, the franchisor has the right to control the corporate identity (appearance) of the franchisee's unit and prescribe the product range. In suitable instances, the franchisor may also offer some technical support, primarily during the early stages of the relationship. However, operational aspects are largely left to the franchisee's discretion. It is easy to see that this can lead to uneven performance by outlets that operate under the same brand but are managed by individuals with their own ideas of how the business should function.

Contrast this with a business format franchise: the franchisee is entitled to receive a corporate identity package, a tried and tested product or service, in-depth training in all aspects of operating the business successfully plus extensive initial and ongoing support. This support is not limited to a little product training but encompasses all facets of operations. The franchisor prescribes the method of doing business and controls every aspect of product/service delivery.

It follows that business format franchising ensures consistency throughout the network because everything has to be done according to the franchisor's proven business model. Not only does this protect the standing of the brand, it also helps franchisees to achieve projected targets of sales and profitability.

The move towards business format franchising received a boost during the late 1940s, again in the USA. At around that time, several things happened which, although seemingly unrelated, combined to drive the growth of franchising.

NEED FOR EXPANSION FINANCE

Changes in lifestyle, linked to the emergence of two-income families, gave a boost to the fast-food segment of the restaurant sector. This triggered the development of a string of quick-service restaurants intended to cater for those who no longer perceived eating out as an occasion but a convenience that would save hassles and time.

Unshackled by traditional ideas, the founders of these new restaurant concepts had turned the sector upside down already. Production line methods had replaced culinary artistry and service was fast and cheerful rather than ceremonial but slow. Although their methods clearly worked, traditional financial channels are notoriously conservative and funding for expansion proved hard to come by.

Emboldened by their early successes and unwilling to spend years proving the merits of what they knew were winning concepts, these new-age entrepreneurs were looking for alternative ways to fund accelerated expansion.

DEMAND FOR OPPORTUNITIES WITH A SAFETY NET

After the end of World War 2, the threat of another world war breaking out had become so remote that the US army embarked on a demobilization drive. This injected a large number of servicemen and women into the economy, mostly ambitious individuals who were eager to make up for lost time by fast-tracking their careers. Many considered entrepreneurship but were reluctant to move ahead with their plans because they lacked essential practical skills.

Although several product format franchises were on offer, they did not provide the necessary support. Reluctant to either undergo training for lengthy periods or risk their demobilization payout on an unproven venture, these ex-soldiers were looking for a more detailed business model.

THE EMERGENCE OF BRAND CONSCIOUSNESS

Increased travel and exposure of a growing number of people to TV advertising were other lifestyle changes that came into play. Consumers wanted to deal with brands they knew they could trust no matter where in the world they happened to be at the time.

Filling a gap in the market

It is in the nature of the free enterprise system that where there is a need someone will come up with a solution. In this case, the development of the business format franchise satisfied the needs I described above. Later in this chapter, I will explain what makes this concept so special but first, let us look at the needs it satisfied.

FAST-FOOD ENTREPRENEURS

The founders of fast-food restaurants had learnt through trial and error how to establish a product offering that satisfies the needs of a changing market. They were now in an excellent position to offer newcomers a tried and tested blueprint for business success.

PROSPECTIVE FRANCHISEES

A large pool of ex-soldiers, keen to start businesses of their own at reduced risk, willingly supplied the necessary cash for the rollout of the brand as well as the necessary commitment to make new outlets successful. In return, they received a comprehensive business model as well as the initial and ongoing support they craved. Another plus factor was that having been soldiers in the past, they were used to following instructions to the letter, so adhering to the franchisor's systems and procedures created no problem for them.

This, by the way, has not changed. Around 2007, the International Franchise Association introduced a scheme aimed at facilitating the integration of war veterans into the mainstream economy. Initially seen as a social responsibility programme, its beneficiaries soon became sought after, with participating franchisors reporting that ex-army personnel make outstanding franchisees.

Insight

Should the requirement of 'following instructions to the letter' put you off franchising, franchising may not be for you but be patient. As franchising evolved, many networks adapted their franchisee profiles to accommodate more entrepreneurial types. Regardless, 'adherence to the system' remains a central requirement and you will read more it in Chapter 2.

CONSUMERS

For the first time ever, consumers were offered an opportunity to patronize their favourite brands at an ever-growing number of locations, initially throughout the USA and later throughout the world. No matter where in the world they happened to find themselves, they could deal with these brands secure in the knowledge that they would receive the range of products and service they had come to expect and love.

How business format franchising works

Several business models exist that appear to function like franchises but essential elements are lacking. On occasion, unscrupulous promoters take advantage of the confusion this creates. Some have succeeded in the past to part the gullible from their money by encouraging them to invest in half-baked or outright fraudulent schemes. It is important, therefore, that you understand the differences fully.

I have already said that a business format franchise is widely seen as a blueprint for business success. It is only logical that this cannot be the case unless the promoter of the franchise has been there, done that successfully and written the book on the subject. Quite literally, actually!

The rights to an idea, no matter how brilliant it might be, should never be presented as a franchise. At best, it could form the basis for the grant of a licence. For a concept to qualify as a business format franchise, the following minimum requirements need to be in place:

▶ *The franchisor has operated the business profitably for a reasonable period. How long is 'reasonable'? Hard to say, but it is generally accepted that the minimum period would be one full year. If seasonal differences are vast, two years may be better.*
▶ *The product is well made and enjoys a high level of demand in a sufficiently large and constantly growing segment of its target market to accommodate additional operators.*
▶ *The systems and procedures required to bring the product to market have been carefully developed and honed to perfection.*
▶ *The franchisor holds the rights over the brand and the brand enjoys the respect of customers, peers and suppliers within the industry sector.*

▶ *The franchisor's know-how has been recorded in an operations and procedures manual. This manual is sufficiently detailed to enable an inexperienced person to operate the business successfully.*

▶ *The franchisor's expansion follows a well thought out plan underpinned by adequate marketing support.*

▶ *The franchisor has access to the necessary funding and is prepared to develop the infrastructure needed to support a growing network of franchisees.*

▶ *The franchisor is committed to ethical franchising and determined to create win–win outcomes between itself and its franchisees.*

LOOK-ALIKES AND IMPOSTORS

Although franchising is not the only route to assisted entrepreneurship, it has become the most successful. The reason for this is that it is the only concept that offers aspiring entrepreneurs a safety net in the form of ongoing support by the franchisor. This does not mean, however, that a franchise is the optimal choice for everyone. Subject to personal preferences, other business models might meet your needs better and you should be familiar with them.

Business opportunity

A business opportunity is precisely what the name suggests, nothing more and nothing less. A manufacturer, importer or wholesaler offers independent entrepreneurs the opportunity to purchase a product at a discount and sell it on at a profit. Individuals who sign up for such an opportunity should expect little, if any, commitment beyond the supply of goods, neither financial nor in the form of ongoing assistance. This type of arrangement is popular in direct selling and can evolve into a multi-level marketing scheme. Sound schemes of this nature have the potential to develop into substantial networks.

On the downside, buyers of business opportunities should not expect to receive much help in the way of training or operational support. Once they have purchased the product, they are essentially on their own but then again, whatever profits they make are theirs to keep. Feedback suggests that some people are doing extremely well out of such schemes. As long as such schemes are presented as what they really are and are not promoted as franchises, I have no problem with them.

Agency agreement

A company appointing an agent (the principal) expects the agent to represent it in negotiations with prospective customers. Business transactions are usually carried out in the name of the principal. On conclusion of the transaction, the company will pay the agent a commission. The agent's investment is limited to the establishment of an office infrastructure and perhaps the financing of local marketing activities. Agency agreements are customary in industrial selling, where the agent maintains good relations with customers and accepts orders. Once the order is placed, however, the goods will be delivered from the principal's factory or warehouse directly to the customer's premises.

Distributorship

A manufacturer, importer or wholesaler establishes a network of independent distributors that will supply goods to end-users. This method of distribution can be utilized at various levels. For the purposes of this book, which essentially looks at the small- and medium-sized enterprises (SME) arena, the most likely scenario would be that of distributors being appointed to sell goods to end-users door to door, either working on their own or with a team of salespeople they employ, usually on a commission basis. The arrangement may entail the payment of an upfront fee in exchange for territorial rights and is sometimes tied to an obligation to purchase a certain amount of stock at regular intervals.

Buying group

A successful retailer creates a loose grouping of established businesses that are independently owned and operated. The chief objective of such arrangements is access to volume discounts. This can be achieved by pooling purchases. On occasion, some branding is involved, giving rise to joint promotions – and confusion regarding their status. They begin to look like franchised networks but in reality, they are not. Examples would be some of the networks of hardware stores and grocery chains that have sprung up over the past few years.

Dealership
This format is widely used by manufacturers of motorcars and other capital items. Dealerships are contracted to sell and service a manufacturer's products, usually on an exclusive basis. They receive some branding and a limited amount of operational support but beyond that, they continue to operate independently.

Beware of pyramid schemes!
If structured properly, the business models discussed up to this point offer legitimate business opportunities. They are not franchises, but then again, not everyone would be happy as a franchisor or franchisee, so they deserve a place in the sun. The same cannot be said for pyramid selling. Pyramid selling schemes are based on deception, plain and simple. This deception comes in the form of an assumption that every investor in a pyramid scheme can sell rights to investors at a lower level in the pyramid. With the best will in the world, this is not sustainable.

This is the reason why pyramid selling has been declared a harmful business practice. This notwithstanding, pyramid selling schemes continue to pop up from time to time, albeit in disguise. They succeed for a while because their promoters' lavish promises appeal to people's greed but in the end, they stand to lose their investment. Do not get taken in by the riches you are promised – unless you are one of the initial promoters, your involvement can only end in tears.

Pyramid selling schemes are usually disguised as distributorships or franchises but in reality, they have nothing in common with either. While any legitimate business model revolves around the sale of a product or the delivery of a service, pyramid selling schemes focus on the granting of territorial rights in return for substantial upfront payments.

The promoters of pyramid selling schemes arbitrarily carve up a country into territories and offer others the right to sell a product within a territory. Inevitably, the product is either entirely useless or hopelessly overpriced. Either way, it is virtually impossible to sell it. This does not bother the promoters, however, because they make their money from the sale of territorial rights.

Those who purchase a territory are entitled to carve it up into smaller territories and sell them to others. This continues until the sub-territories are the size of a city block and hapless 'distributors' are literally tripping over each other. Every one of these transactions involves payments for territorial rights to the holder of these rights who in turn is compelled to pay part of the proceeds to the person who sold him or her the rights; this goes right up the ladder, with the original promoters receiving a share of every transaction that is taking place.

Quite obviously, the promoters of the pyramid scheme as well as those who join the scheme early on stand to make lots of money, but once the momentum runs out, as it must, investors are left with worthless stock and no way to recoup their investment.

Manufacturing franchise

This arrangement entails the granting of a licence by an inventor or patent holder, also known as the licensor, to a manufacturer. The manufacturer, who becomes the licensee, will be authorized to produce a specific product in accordance with the licensor's technical specifications.

Table 1: Typical characteristics of various business models

Description of the business model under consideration	Legal contract	Initial fee	Ongoing fees	Investment details	Initial support	Ongoing support	Right to sell the business
Business opportunity	General	Usually none	Usually none	Stock only	Very limited	None or low	Unfettered
Agency agreement	Detailed			Set-up costs	Substantial	Substantial	
Distributorship	General	None or moderate		Set-up costs, stock and operating capital	Limited training and support	Extremely limited support	
Voluntary chain	General		None or low				
Dealership	Detailed						

Product franchise	Detailed	Relatively high	Low	Substantial training and support	Usually subject to approval of buyer by franchisor
Business format franchise	Very detailed	High		Substantial training and support	
Conversion franchise					

In exchange for granting the licence, the licensor receives either a lump sum or a percentage of the value of the items that are produced. On occasion, a licence provides for a mix of both forms of remuneration, namely a lump sum payable upfront and an ongoing percentage of sales or profits. The licensor may grant technical assistance upfront, and perhaps monitor product quality on an ongoing basis, but is unlikely to offer operational support, nor will he or she control the way in which the licensee conducts its business.

Calling such an arrangement a manufacturing franchise is not fraudulent. Given today's widely accepted interpretation of the word 'franchise', however, the use of the term 'manufacturing franchise' is an unfortunate choice of words and should be avoided. The term 'manufacturing licence' reflects the nature of the relationship far better.

Franchising

The main forms of franchising, namely product (trademark) franchising and business format franchising, have been explained earlier in this chapter. To restate them here would be pointless repetition. The reason why I mention them again is that Table 1 summarizes the most salient characteristics of the business models discussed so far, including franchising.

Conversion franchising

The last item listed in Table 1 is 'conversion franchising'. A conversion franchise is a business format franchise with a minor difference.

In most instances, franchises are established from scratch and operated by a franchisee with little or no prior experience in the sector. Conversion franchising, however, targets established operators in the same sector. In other words, the owner of an established business in the same sector is offered an opportunity to join the network as a franchisee. This involves a conversion of the business into a fully-fledged franchise. In the right circumstances, such a conversion can offer significant advantages to both parties:

SEEN FROM THE FRANCHISOR'S VIEWPOINT:
As the franchisee has an established site and an existing customer base, the franchisor can look forward to gaining market share more rapidly than if the outlet were to be set up from scratch. This will be of interest, for example, if:

▶ *Suitable sites for expansion are difficult to obtain. By admitting the established operator into the network, the franchisor gains a site and eliminates a competitor at the same time.*
▶ *In some industry sectors, discounts offered by suppliers in exchange for bulk orders are substantial. To gain a competitive advantage, the franchisor needs to push up sales as rapidly as possible. Taking in established operators facilitates that.*

SEEN FROM THE FRANCHISEE'S VIEWPOINT:
In highly competitive sectors, for example retail, independent operators are often forced to fight a losing battle against the large chains. By joining a franchise, these operators gain access to the benefits big corporations enjoy while retaining a high degree of independence.

▶ *The independent will typically be attracted by the bulk purchase benefits, advertising muscle and brand recognition the network can offer.*
▶ *Increasingly, access to sophisticated IT systems including website development and e-commerce technology are also becoming major draw cards.*

Check your understanding
Earlier in this chapter, I explained how a product franchise differs from a business format franchise. This is not simply about semantics; the differences between the two concepts are significant. Should you need to choose one business model over the other, a thorough understanding of these differences will be extremely helpful. Before we go any further, let's see whether you can remember them.

Advantages and disadvantages of franchising

In the words of a past president of the International Franchise
Association (IFA), Bill Cherkasky, 'franchising is not perfect but
it is the best blueprint for business expansion that is currently
known. Until someone comes up with something better, it deserves
your wholehearted support.'

I concur with Cherkasky's statement 100 per cent. Franchising
offers many benefits to franchisors and franchisees alike. But while
the concept has much to recommend it, it has some drawbacks as
well. To assist you in forming a balanced view, I will touch on these
from the franchisee's and the franchisor's viewpoint respectively.

Seen from the franchisee's viewpoint

Advantages
PROVEN BLUEPRINT
By investing in a bona fide franchise, the franchisee obtains the right to
a 'blueprint for business success'. He or she can follow this blueprint
with confidence, not only initially but also on an ongoing basis.
It would be reasonable to expect that the time it would ordinarily
take to establish the business, pass the hurdle of 'break-even' and

eventually reach satisfactory levels of profitability will be considerably shorter than if the same business were to be operated independently. Moreover, poor business decisions made because of lack of experience and errors in judgement are practically eliminated.

ESTABLISHED TRADEMARK
Instead of having to establish his or her credentials from scratch, a franchisee benefits from the goodwill that is linked to the network's trademark. In some instances, for example in the service sector, the franchisee will also gain access to the local branches of the network's national customer base.

An example would be cleaning services provided to the head office of a bank by the franchisor. If this bank has a branch in the new franchisee's territory, he or she would stand an excellent chance of obtaining the local cleaning contract. These factors combine to help the franchisee grow the business quickly.

POSSIBLE COST SAVINGS
Although later in this chapter I will classify 'cost' as a negative in evaluating the merits of investing into a franchise, this is not a contradiction. Rather, there are two sides to this equation and both need to be carefully considered. In many industries, the mere fact that the franchisee is able to plug into the franchisor's superior buying power provides cost benefits. Indeed, cases are on record where savings arising from bulk buying are greater than the sum total of ongoing fees franchisees are compelled to pay.

INDUSTRY EXPERIENCE MAY NOT BE NECESSARY
In most franchise concepts, the underlying operations have been simplified and standardized to such an extent that previous industry experience is not an essential requirement. On the contrary, it is sometimes seen as a hindrance. Because it is generally easier to teach a newcomer from scratch than to force an old hand to unlearn bad habits, many franchisors prefer to recruit franchisees with no experience in the industry sector.

This offers a window of opportunity for those people who wish to make a career-change at a later stage in their lives. It could also explain why many people wait until they have reached their forties and fifties before they take the big step.

The franchisee support infrastructure put in place by the franchisor helps franchisees deal with operational problems as they arise. In addition, by utilizing the ongoing support services offered by the franchisor, the franchisee has, in effect, an in-house business consultant at his or her disposal.

But there is more: by joining a franchise, the new franchisee becomes a member of a family. Should a problem arise, he or she has open access to others in the network. It is likely that they have encountered the same problem previously. Because franchisees are usually not in competition with each other, they should be willing to give newcomers the benefit of their experience.

Disadvantages
There are some, but in comparison with the impressive list of advantages they pale into insignificance. No matter, before you make up your mind about joining a franchise you need to be aware of them.

SET-UP COSTS
Set-up costs might be a little higher than if you do things 'on the cheap'. To protect the network's corporate identity, the franchisor will insist that a professional image must be maintained. Although this means that you cannot furnish the store with furniture you found in your parent's attic, it also means that you won't have to replace anything for the next few years. Other considerations come into play as well.

▶ *Prospective customers might place greater trust in a company that looks the part. This in turn might mean that you reach break-even sooner.*
▶ *The franchisor's professional contacts and bulk buying arrangements should ensure that you get a fair deal.*
▶ *Should you need to borrow money from the bank, they will be happier to lend it to you if they can see that you are dealing with approved suppliers.*

FRANCHISE FEES

As a franchisee, you are expected to pay an upfront fee or joining fee as well as ongoing fees. I deal with this more fully in Chapter 3. At this point, let me just say that the right to operate under the network's trademark plus access to training, bulk buying and ongoing support should more than make up for these fees.

OPERATIONAL CONSTRAINTS

Some franchisees consider the operational constraints imposed by the franchise agreement a disadvantage. They also resent the fact that the franchisor exercises close operational control. What they overlook is that every network is only as strong as its weakest link, and it is in their own best interest to comply with procedures that have been proven to work.

STRUCTURAL WEAKNESSES

Under-financed, weak or unprofessional franchisors could have a negative impact on the development of a live-wire franchisee's business. If, for example, the franchisor is less than diligent in building the brand and enforcing compliance with agreed minimum standards throughout the network, the brand's reputation could suffer. This could impact negatively on the value of one franchisee's business, through no fault of his or her own.

Insight

A careful investigation of the franchise opportunity you favour will all but eliminate your risk of joining the wrong network. The steps you need to follow will be set out for you in Chapter 5.

Seen from the franchisor's viewpoint

Advantages

REDUCED CAPITAL NEEDS

Franchisees can be expected to provide the necessary capital for the establishment and operation of the unit they own. It follows that business expansion via the franchising route will absorb less capital than the establishment of branches would require.

RAPID MARKET PENETRATION
Franchisees don't just supply the necessary finance. Because they are owner-operators, they can be relied upon to take care of operational problems at unit level. This reduces the pressure on the franchisor's management team and makes it possible to focus Head Office resources on franchisee support and brand building activities.

RAPIDLY GROWING BUYING POWER
In many instances, rapid expansion of a network leads to a corresponding increase in buying power. This improves the competitiveness of all members of the network and enables the network to gain additional market share.

OPERATIONAL EFFICIENCIES
Owner-operators have been found to be far more effective in everything they do than salaried managers. Companies that have converted branches into franchises report significant increases in sales as soon as operational control shifted from a salaried manager to a franchisee. Almost without exception, this is followed by enhanced profitability soon after.

Insight
It is noteworthy that in some instances, such a turnaround occurred even though the former branch manager had purchased the business and assumed the mantle of franchisee. This proves that owner-operators tend to outperform managers by a considerable margin, even in instances where managers are paid performance bonuses. It also proves that ownership is the highest form of motivation!

ENHANCED INCOME STREAMS
For reasons explained above, franchisees' involvement in the network tends to maximize sales. As franchise fees are usually calculated as a percentage of franchisees' sales, the franchisor's

income increases correspondingly. And because franchise agreements are entered for the long term, financial forecasting becomes more reliable.

BETTER EQUITY POSITION
Loan finance raised by individual franchisees wishing to finance the establishment of their businesses will not be reflected in the franchisor's balance sheet. Only in the unlikely event that the franchisor provides surety for a franchisee would a contingent liability arise.

Disadvantages
The advantages listed above notwithstanding, to franchise a business is not all plain sailing. This step can have disadvantages as well. The implied moral responsibility every franchisor assumes for the welfare of its franchisees must surely top the list of negatives. An entrepreneur who decides to franchise a business no longer just puts his own capital at risk but the franchisees' as well. Some individuals find this a heavy burden to bear. This in turn could make them less willing to exploit additional opportunities because they fear that this may expose franchisees to unacceptable risk, thus slowing down the growth of the brand. Other potential problems arising from franchising are:

HIGH INITIAL COST OF FRANCHISING
Franchising is a numbers game. The more franchisees there are in a network the greater is the likelihood that the franchise operation becomes profitable. This can be explained by the relatively high initial cost involved in creating a franchise package.

▶ *If everything is done professionally, the total cost is likely to be about £35 000. It goes without saying that this cost cannot be recouped from the first franchisee. Rather, it has to be amortized over a period from a large number of franchisees.*
▶ *The infrastructure needed to provide effective franchisee support must be in place from the very beginning, but is likely to remain under-utilized until critical mass has been reached. The definition of critical mass, meaning the number*

of franchisees needed to make a franchise operation profitable,
varies from one industry to the next.

▶ *It is generally accepted that a concept is not franchiseable
unless its promoter has good reason to believe that within
a relatively short period, a minimum of 15 to 25 outlets
can be established. Most franchised networks surpass the
hurdle of 'critical mass' within three to five years after
franchising commenced. At that point, franchising can become
increasingly profitable.*

REDUCED PER-UNIT PROFITABILITY

New franchisors will soon discover that the profit potential of a
well-managed company-owned store is higher than the fee income
a franchised unit generates. The reason for this is simple: Returns
from franchised units are limited to a small percentage of the unit's
sales in the form of franchise fees, while the full profit generated by
a company-owned store will be retained.

This is assuming, of course, that the company-owned store is
operated at peak efficiency. In practice, this rarely happens, unless
one of the owners of the business exercises hands-on control.
A viable solution, applied with increasing frequency, seems to lie in
a mixed approach to expansion.

▶ *Company-owned stores are located in close proximity to the
company's head office, thus permitting hands-on control by
one of the owners.*
▶ *Units located some distance away from head office are
franchised.*

UNDER-PERFORMING FRANCHISEES

In a branch operation, managers who fail to meet agreed targets
can be disciplined or even dismissed. Given that the franchisee has
made a sizeable investment and owns the business, termination of a
franchise agreement, although possible, is far more problematic.

Assuming that a franchisee fails to respond to intensive care
offered by the franchisor and termination remains the only viable

alternative, several aspects including the question of ownership of the business, property lease and loan obligations the franchisee may have entered into must be taken into account. In practice, the franchisor has several alternatives.

▶ *The franchisor could help the franchisee sell the unit.*
▶ *The franchisor can step in, assume responsibility for the failing franchisee's obligations and operate the business as a company-owned unit until a new franchisee can be found.*
▶ *Should the franchisor be unable to facilitate the sale of the unit, and unwilling to take it over, the trade restraint the franchisee will have signed could be waived. This would permit the errant franchisee to continue trading, but outside the network. In this event, every item likely to maintain the impression in the public's mind that the business continues to be a member of the network should be removed promptly.*

Under any one of these scenarios, the repercussions for the former franchisee would be drastic, and negative publicity would be almost inevitable. Should it become clear, therefore, that the failure of the business is not entirely the franchisee's fault, but is the result of poor site selection advice given by the franchisor, some form of compensation might be appropriate.

PROBLEMS SURROUNDING TERRITORIAL PROTECTION
Franchisees and their legal advisors tend to demand territorial protection – an undertaking by the franchisor that no other unit will be opened nearby. Although on the surface of it, this request sounds reasonable enough, acceding to it can create all sorts of problems for the franchisor.

The granting of some form of territorial protection is almost unavoidable in the case of certain service franchises, where an overlap of operations would lead to infighting among franchisees of the same network. On the other hand, retailers and fast-food operators have found that territorial restrictions can become highly counter-productive. By way of example, two or three outlets of the same fast-food brand have been known to co-exist in one large shopping centre. Had the franchisor failed to exploit the opportunity, the opposition would have moved in.

Another problem resulting from the granting of protected territories for service franchises is that at the time the initial expansion strategy is formulated, most franchisors lack the experience needed to assess the true potential of any given area. New franchisors usually tend to err on the side of caution and give away large territories. Provided that the franchisee is sufficiently motivated to exploit the territory and establish additional units as this becomes feasible, this works well enough.

Problems can also arise when a franchisee has reached his comfort zone and is unwilling to expand the business but will not allow the franchisor to place other operators into 'his' territory. Apart from losing potential sales, the network could lose market share to third-party operators who will be quick to fill the need that has been created by the network's marketing campaigns. The best way around this is to keep franchisees' territories relatively small to begin with. This can be linked to an option in the franchisee's favour to expand into neighbouring territories within an agreed period, subject to carefully laid-down performance criteria being met.

In certain circumstances, the granting of territorial protection could be seen as a restrictive practice and raise the ire of the competition authorities. To prevent this from becoming an issue, it is OK for the franchisor to give an undertaking to the effect that it will not place additional units into the protected territory. Should other franchisees within the network decide to ignore agreed boundaries and operate within a fellow-franchisee's territory, the franchisor may be powerless to stop them. If so, this needs to be recorded in the franchise agreement.

LIMITATIONS ON THE FREEDOM TO ACT
In a legal sense, the franchisor will have the power to determine product policy and marketing strategy as well as make any other decisions that affect the direction of the network. Experienced franchisors will rarely take unilateral decisions; they know that franchisees like to be consulted. Moreover, they appreciate that

their franchisees are in constant contact with the network's customers and know what the market wants. It follows that consulting with them will improve the quality of the franchisor's decision-making and enhance franchisees' subsequent buy-in.

On occasion, however, this consultative process might limit the franchisor's flexibility and cause the network to miss an opportunity for growth. An entrepreneurial franchisor may find this difficult to accept, but on balance, it usually works to the long-term advantage of the brand.

DISHONEST FRANCHISEES
When people talk about franchise fraud, they are usually referring to fraudulent franchise schemes. But fraud can be perpetrated by franchisees as well. You will read in Chapter 3 that franchise fees are usually calculated as a percentage of the franchisee's sales. If a crooked franchisee finds a way of under-reporting sales, the franchisor's fee income will be affected.

To eliminate such insidious practices requires a multi-faceted approach:

▶ *The network's systems must be designed in such a way that it is extremely difficult to tamper with them.*
▶ *The franchisor's field service representative should have a sufficiently good grasp of the business's potential to pick up discrepancies.*
▶ *Franchisees should be left in no doubt that should fraudulent practices be discovered, the relevant provisions of the franchise agreement will be invoked. Fee fraud would destroy the trust that forms the basis of any franchise relationship, leaving no room for 'second chances'.*

Franchising's growth continues

Although the fast-food people pioneered franchising, the advantages of franchising are such that other industry sectors were quick to follow their example. Before long, franchising was well on its way to becoming the preferred method of distribution for businesses as diverse as motorcar repair and after-fitment services, home repair and cleaning services, retail, training, tuition and many other sectors. Even medical doctors utilized the concept to set up networks of clinics that offer a range of services to clearly defined niche markets.

In addition to taking US markets by storm, franchising expanded into other parts of the world with ease. What usually happened was that US-based concepts would export their tried and tested systems, usually under a master licence arrangement. It was inevitable that the arrival of a US concept in the target country would attract the attention of local entrepreneurs. Intrigued by what they observed, they set off on a study tour to the USA. Impressed by what they had seen, they would return to their home countries and develop their own networks.

Insight

Franchising's rapid acceptance by various industry sectors that target vastly different markets demonstrates how adaptable the concept is. Although franchising was developed in the USA in response to a local need, entrepreneurs from other parts of the world had no trouble adopting it, generally with great success.

THE EMERGENCE OF FRANCHISE ASSOCIATIONS

The success of franchising prompted a slew of less than ethical operators to enter the sector. Fortunately, they never managed to gain a significant foothold. Much of the credit for the orderly development of franchising must go to the International Franchise Association (IFA). Bill Rosenberg and a few likeminded franchisors founded the IFA in 1961. Originally, its mission was to promote ethical franchising, and this has not changed.

▶ *Soon after its establishment, the IFA published the world's first Code of Ethics and Business Practices for Franchising. Today, the IFA is widely recognized as the world's leading guardian of ethical franchising.*

▶ *Inspired by the activities of the IFA, franchisors in other countries established national franchise associations and by now, over 50 such bodies exist.*

▶ *Many of the national associations are also members of the World Franchise Council, yet another IFA initiative. Moreover, franchisors in Europe established the European Franchise Federation, intended to serve as a forum for pan-European collaboration in the franchise sector.*

Franchising has evolved into a truly global movement, and its continued development appears assured. Chapter 7 of this book contains additional information about the activities of some of the leading national franchise associations and the status of franchising in their respective home countries.

Did you know?

In the UK, franchising has grown into a multi-billion pound industry. According to the 2008 NatWest/BFA survey, the volume of sales achieved through franchised outlets has surpassed the £12 billion mark per annum. Equally impressive is the fact that over 800 franchise systems serve the market through over 34 000 franchisees. The sector provides employment for more than 380 000 people. (These figures reflect the situation in 2007, the latest available at the time of going to press. The website www.natwest.com provides up-to-date information on this topic.)

WHAT CAN BE FRANCHISED?

Given the inroads made by franchising to date, you might wonder what other types of businesses are franchiseable. This is an excellent question but one that is difficult to answer. Some over-enthusiastic proponents of franchising will tell you that every business concept under the sun can be franchised. They are almost right but experience has shown that some sectors franchise better than others. This is influenced by the nature of the product, the status of the market and the organizational culture that prevails in the sector.

It has been found that if the distribution of a product or service requires skills that are in short supply and/or difficult to acquire, this sector is unlikely to franchise well. The potential to generate reasonable profits is another determinant. As you will see in Chapter 3, although franchising is a highly effective distribution concept, it is relatively expensive to implement and control.

In most instances, a business concept is unlikely to prosper as a franchise unless conditions in the market allow for robust trading margins. However, notable exceptions do exist. One example is the retailing of groceries. Although margins are tight, some national grocery chains have evolved into highly successful franchised networks. They have managed to leverage their enormous purchasing power to make up for the cost of operating a franchised network.

The list below summarizes some of the essential characteristics that make a product or service franchiseable. (To enhance readability, the term 'product' has been used throughout. Please note that in the case of a service, the same basic considerations would apply.)

Characteristics that make a product or service franchiseable

▶ *The product is of good quality and likely to generate repeat demand.*
▶ *The product is marketed under a reputable brand. Alternatively, realistic potential to create a brand exists. (Not only does brand building require large amounts of money, in the case of a basic commodity, it would be difficult to achieve.)*
▶ *The target market is well established, of reasonable size and has the potential to grow further.*
▶ *The product has staying power; demand is neither highly seasonal nor associated with a short-term fad.*
▶ *Ruling market forces allow for reasonable mark-ups. Moreover, in the eyes of the product's primary target market, price is less important than brand association and service excellence.*

- ▶ *Access to raw materials and production capacity is assured and no other supply constraints are known to exist.*
- ▶ *Should the effective distribution of the product be highly site dependent, access to such sites in sufficient numbers is assured.*
- ▶ *It is relatively easy to pass on the know-how a new franchisee needs to acquire, and an average individual with little or no prior experience in the sector can absorb it within a reasonable training period.*
- ▶ *Processes have been adequately recorded within one or more operations manuals and operations are adequately systemized to allow the franchisee to duplicate the franchisor's success.*

What does the future hold?

Given the rapid advance of franchising over the past five decades, you might wonder when the movement will hit a brick wall. I can assure you that franchising is far from reaching saturation point, as the following facts show:

- ▶ *In the USA, franchising currently accounts for about 50 per cent of all retail sales. The current economic downturn has slowed down expansion somewhat but when the economy turns, franchised networks will be in better shape to take advantage of it than independents who may have gone out of business.*
- ▶ *The franchise sector in other countries holds 10 to 25 per cent of retail sales. This in itself is an indication of the sector's potential for growth.*
- ▶ *The number of industry sectors that expand through franchising can be expected to grow as well. Although food concepts will remain among the leaders in the franchise sector, it will never again be their exclusive domain. This does not mean that food franchises are in decline. Rather, it means that an ever-growing number of industry sectors will adopt franchising as their preferred vehicle for expansion.*

Franchise guides lists concepts as diverse as the installation of fire places, travel services, pest control services, snacks distributors, professional photography and film processing among the numerous franchise opportunities on offer. Given this bewildering range of opportunities, it should not surprise you that investment levels vary widely as well. In the actual examples I have mentioned above, the total investment required ranges from £7000 all the way to £45 000.

Other opportunities require investments going into hundred thousands of Pounds; several websites including www.whichfranchise.com (for England) and its sister sites the world over list opportunities complete with indication of investment levels; for details see Chapter 7. I will deal more with the financial aspects of franchising in Chapter 3.

Insight

Perhaps you are the owner of a successful business that is ready for expansion, or you are an individual looking for a business opportunity with a safety net? Whatever your circumstances, you should at least consider franchising as an expansion tool. Its track record speaks for itself.

THE TEN MOST IMPORTANT THINGS YOU NEED TO REMEMBER

1 *In most countries, the use of the word 'franchise' is not controlled by government degree. The mere fact that someone calls something a franchise does not make it so. The onus is on you to investigate whether all the required ingredients for a successful franchise are in place.*

2 *Even if a franchise is a fully-fledged business format franchise, it does not come with any guarantees. Like every business venture, a franchise contains an element of risk. Ultimately, success or failure depends on the franchisee's ability, dedication and willingness to adhere to the blueprint.*

3 *Should you decide to invest in a product franchise, you cannot expect to receive the same level of support as a business format franchise offers. On the other hand, a product franchise offers a less controlled environment. Only you can decide what suits you best.*

4 *Although entrepreneurs in the quick service restaurant sector were the first to offer franchises, franchising is no longer limited to this sector. Franchise opportunities are now offered in almost every industry sector imaginable. As long as the concept addresses the needs of an established and growing market, profit margins are reasonable and the necessary know-how is relatively easy to transfer, the concept can usually be franchised.*

5 *An idea can never be franchised. The whole point of investing in a franchise and paying fees to the franchisor is to obtain access to a brand and a tried and tested business system.*

6 *New entrepreneurs love franchising because they know that the free enterprise system can be a hard taskmaster. While entering the world of business under a franchise does not guarantee success, it makes it easier to succeed if you operate under the umbrella of an established brand from day one.*

7 *Owners of established businesses love franchising because they can expand their businesses at a much faster pace than would otherwise be possible. This is because franchisees invest their own funds into the venture and are committed towards making the business successful. This reduces the need for start-up capital, improves productivity and enhances the level of service consumers enjoy.*

8 *Consumers love franchised outlets because it protects them from the unknown. If a consumer travels abroad or moves to a new town, he or she finds comfort in the fact that the brand they have come to trust remains accessible to them.*

9 *Franchising is not without its pitfalls, with the interdependence between franchisor and franchisee heading the list. If, for example, a franchisor wishes to implement a major change in strategy, chances are that this will affect franchisees' interests. This may limit the franchisor's ability to exploit opportunities. Franchisees, on the other hand, are contractually bound to adhere to the network's blueprint. They must also accept that the network's interests will always rank above their own self-interests.*

10 *While franchising is the most successful business model ever developed, it is not entirely immune to economic downturns. However, it stands to reason that a member of an established network has a better chance of negotiating the rough currents of a slump in the economy better than an independent operator and recover faster once the tide turns.*

2

The central characters in the franchise relationship

In this chapter you will learn:
- *what it takes to become an entrepreneur*
- *in which ways becoming a franchisee differs*
- *what it takes to become a franchisor*
- *what other stakeholders are affected*

Now that you know how franchising works and what the concept's potential is, the time has come to turn to the human factor. In this chapter, you will find answers to the following questions:

▶ *What does it take to become a franchisee?*
▶ *What does it take to become a franchisor?*
▶ *What is the consumer's interest in all this?*

What does it take to become a franchisee?

After five decades of rampant growth, franchising's effectiveness as a tool for business creation and expansion is no longer in doubt. But no matter how well franchising works for others, unless the franchise you join meets your expectations, success is likely to elude you. I suggest that before you embark on the epic journey towards operating your own franchise, you need to establish what it is you expect to get out of the arrangement.

THE DREAM VERSUS THE REALITY

It is not at all unusual for people to dream of starting a business some day and for many it remains just that – an idle dream. Others become involved in shaky ventures and have their dreams shattered by the grim realization that being your own boss is not all that it's cracked up to be.

> **Insight**
>
> After a stint in self-employment that ended in financial distress, a failed entrepreneur was overheard muttering to himself: 'I quite enjoyed being my own boss. What spoiled it for me was the fact that I had to be my own employee.'

How can you make sure that you end up with a business that is everything you have always wanted? Realistically speaking, you can't! No matter how carefully you prepare for your entry into entrepreneurship, an element of risk remains, even if it is a franchise. Anyone who tells you otherwise is either dishonest or a fool. However, there is a lot you can do to protect yourself against making wrong choices by doing your homework first. Although it won't guarantee the success of your business, or your personal happiness, you will at least know what you let yourself in for.

ESSENTIAL PREREQUISITES

Before you even consider whether becoming a franchisee would suit you, you need to understand that regardless of whether you join a franchised network or go it alone, many of the essential prerequisites for success as an entrepreneur remain the same. These include:

► *Passion for the product or service;*
► *A willingness to work hard;*
► *An obsession with service excellence;*
► *Good communication skills;*
► *Patience, optimism, decisiveness, determination and commitment;*

- ▶ *The ability to act responsibly at all times;*
- ▶ *Plenty of organizational talent;*
- ▶ *Excellent health;*
- ▶ *Access to adequate finance and the ability to handle money responsibly;*
- ▶ *Access to a strong support network (family, friends, etc.).*

To round this off, you should be a self-starter with a knack for bouncing back when things go wrong and an innate ability to keep a cool head in the face of a looming crisis. In addition, you need to possess certain core competencies, including:

- ▶ *Strong marketing orientation;*
- ▶ *Outstanding people skills;*
- ▶ *Excellent problem-solving abilities;*
- ▶ *The ability to focus on the minutest detail without losing sight of the bigger picture;*
- ▶ *A high level of business ethics.*

WHAT IS YOUR MOTIVATION?

People start businesses for a variety of reasons. It is important that you know what drives you to take this step. Is it because you want to control your own destiny? Be able to implement your own ideas? Become extremely rich? Be your own boss because it means that nobody can tell you what to do? Be able to boss others around?

Researchers tell me that the most frequent answer is 'To make lots of money!' This sounds reasonable enough, but be careful. These same researchers also found that while money can be an important motivator, making money, even lots of it, usually fails to keep a person motivated for very long.

Another interesting finding is that those respondents who lack passion for the work they are doing generally perform badly and the great riches they had been hoping for are unlikely to materialize. Contrast this with the experiences of those entrepreneurs who are passionate about their businesses. They cannot wait to get to work in the mornings, love every minute of every working day and their passion shines through. As a result, they create profits almost by default.

FRANCHISE-SPECIFIC CHARACTERISTICS

The above considerations are important if you want to start your own business, regardless of whether you plan to invest in a franchise or go it alone. Should you elect to go the franchise route, however, some additional requirements need to be taken into consideration.

A solid understanding of franchising
A sound knowledge of the franchise concept will help you to understand what life as a franchisee might be like. This should minimize the danger of unwanted surprises cropping up at a later stage.

The patience to investigate properly
As soon as you have decided that franchising is the route you want to take, you need to take a step back. Rushing out to investigate the various franchise opportunities on offer is exciting, but you need to take it one step at a time.

▶ *Do an in-depth investigation of the market sector you are interested in.*
▶ *Talk to several franchisors active in this sector and find out what the advantages and disadvantages of their respective franchise offerings are.*
▶ *Only once you have gained a sound understanding of the industry sector you are interested in should you begin to focus on one specific franchise opportunity.*

Insight
You should never be in a hurry to sign a franchise agreement. Before you do that, you need to find out everything there is to know about the network. A franchise is a long-term arrangement. You owe it to yourself to make the right choice.

I have compiled detailed guidelines for the evaluation of a franchise opportunity in Chapter 5 and advise you to refer to them often.

Willingness to follow the system

Are you willing to comply with the requirements of a franchise system, even if you think you know a better way to do things? A franchisor's instructions are usually very detailed and you will be expected to follow them. Should you disagree with something, you cannot change it as you please. However, most experienced franchisors encourage input from franchisees and have a process in place to facilitate this. But they also reserve the right to accept or reject it as they see fit. Unless you can live with that, a franchise might not be the best option for you.

Adequate funding

As franchisee, you will be responsible for raising the necessary finance, firstly, to establish your unit, and secondly, to fund its ongoing operation. Of course, this requirement is not specific to franchising – it would apply to any business start-up situation. Seeing that you have to pay an upfront fee and follow the franchisor's guidelines when you fit out your unit, you might need more capital upfront than if you go it alone. What balances the equation somewhat is the fact that banks are generally happier to deal with a franchisee of an approved franchisor rather than an entrepreneur who is about to start an unproven venture from scratch.

Receptiveness to new ideas

To make it in the increasingly competitive business arena, you need to be receptive to new ideas and able to grasp new concepts quickly. Once again, this applies to any business format but becomes even more important if you join a franchise. Franchised networks tend to be highly innovative organizations – this is what turns them into market leaders in the first place – and expect their franchisees to keep up.

Willingness to accept criticism

As a franchisee, you need to be willing to accept advice and constructive criticism from members of the franchisor team. If you think about it, this is not a bad thing. The franchisor has experience on its side and your best interest at heart. They don't do that for philanthropic reasons, mind you, but because they know that the success of the network depends on the rate of success its franchisees achieve. That's what turns franchising into a win–win concept.

Single-mindedness

Your franchisor will expect you to focus on the business and exploit its potential to the fullest. Should you have many interests outside the business, it might make you a more interesting conversationalist but it would also distract you from operating the business. This could cause tension with the franchisor and you could even find yourself in breach of the franchise contract.

Insight

Senior franchise executives at McDonald's often joke that when they accept a new franchisee into the fold, the training period includes a visit to the in-house operating theatre. In this facility, the franchisee receives a blood transfusion of sorts. Blood is replaced with McDonald's proprietary brand of tomato ketchup.

Being a team player

To make the grade as a franchisee, you need to be a team player.

▶ *You need to accept that the brand comes first, even if it means that you have to subordinate your personal goals for a while. In the long term, the interests of the brand should never be in competition with your own interests. If they are, you have made a poor choice.*
▶ *You will be expected to make a meaningful contribution to the ongoing growth of the network. This means, among other things, that you need to be willing to share your ideas, successes and failures freely with the franchisor's team and your peers. Unless you are willing to participate fully in all network-wide activities, you might soon find yourself isolated. The 'lone ranger' type is unlikely to ever reap the full benefits a franchised network has to offer.*

Health issues and family support

There is no doubt in my mind that the factors I have listed above are important. Even if they are all in place, however, it will account for little unless you are naturally energetic and in excellent health. And your secret weapon will be the backing of your family.

Regardless of whether you expect close family members to work in the business or not, in some way or other, they will be affected and deserve to be consulted. Once you are in the thick of it, their willingness to provide you with a comfort zone and offer moral support will be invaluable. Should such support not be forthcoming, your life is likely to be sheer hell.

Test yourself
Having browsed through the above points, you might feel that you have what it takes to become a successful franchisee. This is great, but not so fast! Given the importance of the step you intend to take, a good feeling alone is simply not enough. To get closer to reality, you need to ask yourself a series of structured questions. Below you will find a questionnaire – complete it and you will have a much better idea of how you shape up.

Important note: I cannot claim that this questionnaire has been scientifically designed. Based on my experience, the questions it contains will indicate your success chances as a franchisee. When you formulate your answers, remember that this is a confidential exercise. Nobody else needs to see your answers unless you want to share them with someone you trust. It would make scant sense, therefore, to be less than honest – that would amount to cheating yourself!

One more thing: Most people find unbiased self-evaluation extremely difficult. Should you be uncertain about your real strengths and weaknesses, or want to have your assessment independently confirmed, I advise you to make photocopies of the questionnaire before you fill it in and ask trusted friends or a loved one to assess you. You need to point out that they will do you no favours by being less than realistic, it will be much better if they rate you as they see you.

By comparing your own findings with the feedback you receive from others, you will gain valuable insights into your personality and the way you project yourself. It might also highlight strengths you were not even aware of, and/or weaknesses you might be able to address. Whatever you do, don't become defensive! Remember that your reviewers merely tried to help. Should you feel that their comments are a bit harsh, consider the possibility that they discovered something about you that you overlooked. By accepting their constructive criticism in the spirit it was presumably given, you are likely to grow as a person.

Self-evaluation: Part A

Aspect under consideration	No problem	Needs work	Problem area
Personal characteristics and attributes			
Am I prepared to work harder than I have ever worked before?			
Am I sufficiently motivated to work without supervision?			
Am I prepared to cut back on my social life, at least during the early years?			
Am I able to cope with the consequences of having to work unsociable hours?			

Am I willing to accept
the need to cut back on
discretionary spending
and holidays for the first
few years after start-up?

Am I of the right age to
start a business (not too
young – possible lack of
experience, not too
old – possible lack of
energy)?

Am I sufficiently fit and
energetic to stand the
course?

Am I healthy enough to
cope with the pressures of
running my own business?

Am I a positive person and
confident in my ability to
succeed?

Personal working style

Do I enjoy working with
people?

Do I generally trust people
and expect the best from
them until proven wrong?

Do I enjoy training others
and seeing them grow as
individuals?

Do I readily acknowledge the contribution made by others?

Do I comprehend that once in business, the buck will stop with me, every time?

Do I enjoy multi-tasking encompassing everything from the menial to the cerebral?

Do I have the ability to motivate others, willing them to succeed?

Do I enjoy delegating tasks to others and letting them get on with the job?

Do I strive for the highest possible standards of excellence in everything I do?

Do I expect others to conform to the highest possible standards of excellence in everything they do?

Do I keep calm under pressure, even if those around me are losing their heads?

My conduct as a business owner

Do I believe implicitly in the premise that the customer is always right?

Do I feel the need to turn my business into the best of its kind in the area?

Do I believe that my business's strongest assets are the brand and its people, in that order?

Family involvement

Have I told them of my plans and how they are likely to impact on their lives?

Are they prepared to share my dream with me?

Do I expect family members to work in the business and how do they feel about it?

Even if they are not directly involved in the business, will they support me anyway?

My life as a franchisee

Do I fully understand how franchising works, and what its success factors are?

Do I realize that the responsibility for the success of my business remains mine?

Do I really accept the need for compliance with the network's guidelines?

Do I see the advantages of being part of a network and does this appeal to me?

Do I plan to participate actively in the network's activities?

Do I accept that being a franchisee means placing group interests above my own?

Do I recognize the need for constant change and renewal?

Self-evaluation: Part B

- What am I good at? List your strongest points – you should aim for at least five. Tip: Don't just list skills that are strictly work-related, list anything that comes to mind. For example, if your favourite hobby is deep-sea diving, list it – you might have a future as the owner of a diving school.

- Now list five things you are bad at. This is important because you would obviously avoid going into a business that involves doing something you are likely to struggle with.

Keep in mind that although as the owner of a business, you will be able to delegate the execution of some tasks, you nevertheless need to exercise overall control. If, for example, you absolutely hate working with figures, you can hire a bookkeeper to record the figures but you still have to keep a tab on figures relating to sales, productivity and financial performance.

Why do I really want to own a business?

- Don't limit yourself to giving what you think are the right answers. Rather, allow yourself the freedom to list whatever comes to mind. If it's something along the lines of 'the freedom to do as I please' or 'making oodles of money', write it down.

- Next, list the reasons why you believe that a franchise is more likely to help you achieve these targets than an independently operated business would.

As long as you answer realistically, discrepancies between your dream and the reality a franchise can offer you will soon show up.

What are my long-term goals?

- List five things you want to achieve in life, and put a timeline to them.

- Ask yourself how operating a franchise is likely to help you achieve your goals within the allotted timeframe.

On completion of this exercise, you will have a good idea whether entrepreneurship is right for you and if so, whether a franchise is the most promising option. Should you fail to find significant synergies, it would be better for you to look elsewhere.

What does it take to become a franchisor?

To franchise a business is a massive undertaking; to provide detailed guidelines for the implementation of a franchise project would exceed the parameters of this book by a wide margin. However, the following text will answer the basic question: 'Is my business franchiseable?' Should you conclude that this is indeed the case, you will find the information contained in the balance of this book extremely useful, but additional resources will be needed. Chapter 7 contains lists of useful contacts and other references.

Is my business franchiseable?

12 critical success factors

When you assess the viability of your existing business for expansion through franchising, you need to consider several critical factors. To aid you in your decision-making process, we have condensed these factors into a series of questions you should be able to answer in the affirmative before you consider franchising your business.

1 *Does the business operate in a large and growing market? Market demand must be sufficient to sustain a franchised network, or even more than one franchise, since competition will inevitably enter the marketplace. A large market will contribute to promising margins, making it an attractive business opportunity for prospective franchisees. The market must also provide room for future growth. The franchisee must be able to grow his or her business in the existing market. And because the profitability of franchising relies on*

a multiplier effect, you should be able to grow the franchise network relatively quickly to make the franchise operation profitable.

2 Is the growth in the market likely to be sustainable? The market must have the potential to grow for a long period, since franchisees usually sign a long-term contract and you as the franchisor will have to build a solid infrastructure to support your franchisees. It follows that fads are not suitable for franchising, since their growth is not sustainable over the long term. Before you embark on a franchise venture, you should test the concept for a reasonable period, preferably in several locations with different demographics and throughout all seasons of the year. This is the only way to prove the concept's feasibility over the long term.

3 Are the margins sufficient to cover the proposed management services fees? The margins must be sufficient to allow the franchisee to achieve an acceptable return on investment over a reasonable period. Projections must take into account that the franchisee has to pay initial and ongoing franchise fees. If franchisees are not able to afford that, the business is simply not franchiseable. To calculate viability, financial projections must be made which are based on existing operations. In a difficult economic climate, it is especially important to demonstrate that the franchisee will be able to repay debt, cover management services fees and is left with some profit.

4 Can the product demand a price premium? Consumers must be willing to pay a price premium for the product in return for added value, for example convenience or exceptional service. Product categories that are caught in price wars do not franchise well. In such instances, there is very little loyalty to the product and margins are likely to remain under constant pressure. In such conditions, franchisees are unlikely to prosper and neither will the network.

5 Does the franchisor have access to sufficient capital? Every franchisor needs capital to finance the pilot phase (market testing), develop the franchise package and build the necessary infrastructure. The first few stages of franchising are capital

intensive. To ensure financial survival, the franchisor needs to be financially stable. Moreover, the franchisor must be able to afford franchising in a professional way. This includes investing in technology and retaining professional assistance. The effect of running out of money midway through the development stage could be catastrophic. You need to consider this when you investigate the viability of franchising.

6 Does the potential exist to establish a memorable brand? The great franchises of the world are also recognized as great brands. Think about Kentucky Fried Chicken and McDonald's. Moreover, famous brands tend to make the move into franchising with ease. For example, Häagen-Dazs, the ice-cream people, opened a chain of cafés on a franchise basis. The criteria for building a brand include uniqueness and the ability to cultivate enduring consumer loyalty. A good brand is easily recognizable and pronounced; this helps consumers to remember it. This is what branding is all about: occupying the number one spot in a consumer's mind to ensure repeat sales. Another important consideration is whether the brand name can be protected effectively. Intellectual property must be registered as soon as possible and should be difficult to copy. Generic names are difficult to register. For example, 'The Coffee Place' is a generic name and would be difficult to protect. 'Joe's Coffee Place', on the other hand, is attached to a person's name and much easier to defend.

7 Is there a substantial barrier to entry, making it difficult to copy the concept? A certain level of uniqueness is one of the prerequisites for a franchiseable concept. A concept that can be copied easily may find it difficult to gain a competitive advantage. Some market sectors are competitive by nature. However, the barrier to entry can be raised by offering consumers advantages other brands are reluctant to match. A good example is tyre fitment centres, usually highly price competitive. By adding services such as extended business hours or a mobile service, operators in this sector can differentiate themselves. This moves the focus away from price.

8 *Will the franchisor's development costs permit a satisfactory return on investment? The franchisor and the franchisee must both be able to achieve a satisfactory return on their respective investments. After all, the franchisor will incur costs linked to the development of the franchise network and the associated infrastructure. The returns the network generates must justify this.*

9 *Is it possible to grow a franchise culture in the company? A franchise culture can be defined as 'open and learning-orientated'. It must be inherently flexible and supportive towards its franchisees. When an organization chooses to go the franchise route, it must be committed to creating win–win situations. After all, the franchisor and the franchisee will depend on each other for their success. On occasion, corporates make poor franchisors because they find it difficult to accommodate the typical entrepreneurial spirit and way of thinking. When a corporation decides to franchise, senior management must accept that franchisees cannot be treated in the same way as branch managers. Franchisees need guidance and support in a flexible and nurturing environment. We like to describe it as leadership rather than dictatorship.*

10 *Does the concept have staying power? A professional franchisor has a long-term commitment to the success of the concept. This includes having a vision for the future of the concept and a strategy designed to ensure continued success. Franchisors must practise the highest business ethics, especially since franchisees trust them with a sizeable investment.*

11 *Is it relatively easy to transfer the required skills? The need for professional qualifications or long training periods might dissuade promising prospects from taking up the opportunity.*

12 *Are suitable systems and procedures in place? This is vital, firstly, to help franchisees maximize operating efficiencies within their units, secondly, to enable the franchisor to assist franchisees in every facet of profitable operations. Franchising is the art of controlled duplication. Without the necessary systems in place, this cannot be implemented effectively.*

Adapted from work done jointly with my colleague Eric J. Parker in the past; reproduced with permission.

Summary

The important question 'Is a franchise the most suitable option?' needs to be answered in two parts.

▶ *Seen from a prospective franchisee's viewpoint, basic prerequisites are:*
  ▷ *The genuine desire to 'operate a business of your own but not on your own', including preparedness to follow instructions;*
  ▷ *The necessary temperament, aptitude and physical stamina to succeed in the business;*
  ▷ *The ability to raise the necessary funding.*
▶ *Seen from a prospective franchisor's viewpoint, basic prerequisites are:*
  ▷ *A careful investigation has revealed that the business meets most if not all of the accepted criteria for franchising;*
  ▷ *The organizational climate that prevails within the company allows a franchise culture to be established;*
  ▷ *Adequate resources are available to ensure that the necessary infrastructure can be put in place and kept operating at peak performance level until the franchise operation becomes self-funding. This will typically require a commitment stretching over three to five years.*

Other stakeholders

The major role players in a franchise are the franchisor and the franchisees within the network, no doubt about that. Such is the complexity of the franchise relationship, however, that other parties are affected as well.

SUPPLIERS

If the franchise involves the purchase of goods for processing and/or resale, the franchisor will usually approach key suppliers to set up network-wide supply arrangements. This means that every franchisee gains access to preferential deals. This is not unlike the situation in a branch operation, with one important difference.

Insight

Although contract provisions will see to it that the franchisor cannot be held responsible for the franchisee's debts, and vice versa, one franchisee's poor payment performance will affect the network's reputation among suppliers. It is for this reason that a good franchisor will not tolerate poor payment performance.

In dealings with a branch network, its head office will be the supplier's main contact point. In a franchise, on the other hand, each franchisee must be treated as an individual customer. It is not surprising, therefore, that the supplier will expect the franchisor to accept at least moral responsibility for franchisees' adherence to the terms and conditions of the supply arrangement.

CUSTOMERS

Given half a choice, companies and individuals alike prefer to deal with the owner of a business; in a franchised network, every branch is operated by its owner. But because the branches trade under the same brand, customers expect each branch to live up to the brand's promise. Should customers experience disappointment at a specific branch, it would not only impact negatively on the unit in question but on all units operating under the same brand.

THE TEN MOST IMPORTANT THINGS YOU NEED TO REMEMBER

1 *Every worthwhile venture starts with a dream, so dreaming is OK – for a while. Collection of all the salient facts comes next and then its time to act, prudently yet decisively.*

2 *Although a franchise is a blueprint for business success, it does not come with guarantees. Willingness to follow the blueprint and work hard on its implementation will help you to become successful.*

3 *To be happy as an entrepreneur, you need to think ahead. Ditch the rose-tinted glasses and investigate what you are going to get into before making a firm commitment.*

4 *Franchising is the most successful business concept known to man but it is not right for everyone. Make sure that you can live with the restrictions the concept imposes on you.*

5 *To enter into a franchise arrangement is a long-term commitment. If you rush into it without thinking it through first, you may find out the hard way that the cost of getting out can be prohibitive.*

6 *Funding is available but trying to set up as a franchisee without capital of your own is a recipe for disaster and no responsible franchisor will be a party to it. Repayments may cripple the new business's cash flow to such an extent that it may fail before you had a sporting chance to prove your mettle.*

7 *To find out what life as a franchisee of a specific network will be like, ask the franchisor to let you work in one of their units for a few days. You won't be paid a salary but the experience will be invaluable.*

8 *Almost everything that has been said above applies equally to an entrepreneur who wants to expand an existing successful business through franchising. Be especially mindful of the fact that changing course mid-stream is not the easiest thing to do.*

9 *A franchisor cannot 'wing it'. Franchisees are buying experience, unless the franchisor has operated the business and made a success of it, there can be no franchise.*

10 *In addition to adequate funding, a new franchisor needs plenty of patience. Experience has shown that it takes three to five years for a new franchise system to become profitable.*

3

Financial aspects of franchising

In this chapter you will learn:
- *what the financial implications of franchising are*
- *how franchise fees are calculated*
- *why compulsory purchase arrangements make sense*
- *how to secure finance for a franchise*

Now that you understand the basic principles of franchising, the time has come to look at its financial implications. I have already said that franchising is a business tool, nothing more and nothing less. It follows that the decision to become involved should make commercial sense. Otherwise, why bother?

Insight

At the outset, a word of caution: Franchising is not, and will never be, a convenient shortcut to quick and easy riches. Regardless of whether you are a prospective franchisee or franchisor, unless you are prepared to take a long-term view, you are likely to be disappointed.

Typical financial obligations

While it is widely accepted that to become a franchisee calls for a substantial investment, the financial obligations of a prospective franchisor are generally less well understood. This can lead to unrealistic expectations, followed by disillusionment with franchising, for no sound reason.

▶ *As a prospective franchisee, the onus is on you to provide the necessary capital. The franchisor will ordinarily not fund your operation but might be willing to facilitate access to grantors of finance.*

▶ *As a prospective franchisor, you need to understand that to deliver on the inherent promise of franchising, you need to make a substantial investment upfront.*

With this in mind, let us look at the financial obligations of both parties, beginning with the prospective franchisee.

THE FRANCHISEE'S FINANCIAL OBLIGATIONS

As a franchisee, your financial obligations can be broken down into five main categories:

1 *Initial franchise fee*
2 *Establishment costs*
3 *Operating costs (working capital)*
4 *Ongoing franchise fees*
5 *Other franchise-related financial obligations.*

Overview

Upon joining a franchise, you will be expected to pay an initial fee. You also need to fund setting-up costs and provide working capital. On an ongoing basis, you are obliged to pay a management services fee and a contribution to the network's marketing fund. Depending on the range of services offered by the franchisor, sundry other fees may become payable as well. Franchise fees, and how they are usually calculated, will be discussed in detail later in this chapter.

Of course, a franchisee is also responsible for all the normal business expenses any business owner has to cover. Examples are rent and utility bills, staff salaries and wages, suppliers' bills, the repayment of bank loans and so on. In this way, a franchise is no different from any other business.

Lastly, don't forget your family's living expenses. Many prospective franchisees are tempted to ignore this aspect, or plan to make do with the bare necessities until the business can afford to pay them a realistic salary. Depending on your personal circumstances, this might not work too well and it is better to be realistic here.

Perhaps the question 'why go the franchise route?' should be asked and answered once more. Joining a properly structured franchise will provide financial benefits, for example in the form of bulk purchase arrangements or joint advertising programmes. Moreover, the time it takes to reach break-even should be shorter because you operate your business under a brand name that already has a following.

Insight

In conversations with franchisees, one point became abundantly clear. As long as you select the right franchise and use the franchisor's support services to the fullest, the financial benefits of operating under a franchise more than offset the extra operating costs in the form of franchise fees.

THE FRANCHISOR'S FINANCIAL OBLIGATIONS

If you have paid attention so far, you will know that before a business can be franchised it needs to have an established brand and a solid track record. But this in itself, although essential, is not enough. The long-term success of a franchised network depends on the quality of its dedicated franchisee support infrastructure. To provide detailed guidelines for the creation of this infrastructure would exceed the parameters of this book. All I can say is that the creation and proper implementation of a franchise project requires a substantial investment upfront. Consider the following needs:

1 *Product-specific market research*
2 *Development and testing of products*
3 *Development and testing of business processes*

4   *Development/fine-tuning of the corporate identity*
5   *Research into the feasibility of franchising*
6   *Preparation of the franchise package including professional fees*
7   *Franchise marketing and recruitment costs.*

Development costs

Expanding a business through franchising can be highly profitable in the long term. Initially, however, expenses are likely to exceed potential income by a wide margin. Unless realistic projections indicate that the franchise will become viable over time, there is no point continuing along this path.

The preparation of the franchise package entails the drafting of the necessary documentation. At a minimum, this entails the drafting and printing of:

▶ *Operations and procedures manual.*
▶ *Financial projections covering the operations of the franchise organization as well as the financial viability of franchised units under various market conditions.*
▶ *Disclosure document. This is obligatory in many countries although currently not in the UK. However, forward-looking franchisors will produce it because well-informed prospects tend to make better franchisees.*
▶ *Franchise agreement. While at a push, all other documentation can be drawn up internally, the franchise agreement needs to be drafted by a solicitor with proven franchise experience.*

You also need to develop franchisee selection criteria and fine-tune your site selection criteria. The development of the franchise marketing plan follows next. Those who have done it will tell you that at this point, professional fees alone will add up to a tidy sum. Add to this the cost of travel, printing and advertising and it becomes obvious that the amount of money you need to set aside for this purpose will be substantial.

In any event, development costs are only part of the total cost of establishing a franchise. Unless you create the necessary infrastructure to attract, evaluate and train prospective franchisees and ease them into their businesses, your franchise is unlikely to take off. This means thorough training of every new franchisee and his or her staff, assistance with site selection and hands-on assistance throughout the process of getting the unit ready to trade. It is followed by the need to provide extensive opening assistance and regular ongoing support. As you cannot be in several places at once, it means that you have to hire competent staff, yet another considerable expense.

Be aware of this trap

When doing their projections, inexperienced franchisors tend to overlook the fact that during the start-up period, all franchisees' businesses will be new. This means that at the time when they require the highest level of support, their sales figures, and with it income from franchise fees, will be at its lowest. See box below.

Insight

As new franchisees come on board, they will require a disproportionate amount of support without generating much in the form of fee income. Every franchisor needs to budget for the resulting cash flow deficit. Eventually, economies of scale will make franchising highly attractive but this does not happen overnight. For example, one field service representative (a term explained in Chapter 6), can be expected to support between 15 and 20 established franchisees. During the early stage of the development of a new network, however, he or she may be hard-pressed to cope with the needs of three or four franchisees. The reason for this is that they are all start-ups and likely to require lots of handholding.

Income from initial fees

The inflow of initial franchise fees, explained later in this chapter, will relieve the pressure on the franchisor's finances somewhat. To rely on these payments for the financial survival of the franchisor operation would be unwise, however, because initial fees are a 'once off windfall'. This income stream depends on the development of additional territories and once network expansion is complete, it will dry up altogether. In the interim, the rate at which initial fees accrue may depend on factors beyond the franchisor's control. Examples are a possible shortage of suitable prospects or lack of access to suitable sites.

This raises yet another point. Should the network's financial survival depend on an ongoing income stream from initial fees, the temptation to 'sell' franchises almost indiscriminately would be great. This could result in sound guidelines for site selection and the selection of franchisees being ignored.

Insight

It is clear that to admit weak franchisees into the network and/or to permit them to operate from poor locations is a recipe for disaster. In business, bad news travels fast and the failure of even one outlet can impact negatively on the network's development.

Why franchise?

I started this chapter with the assertion that going the franchise route must make commercial sense. Now I am telling you that it costs lots of money to go this route, and will take a long time, typically three to five years, to begin to pay off for you. Just in case you are beginning to get cold feet, let us look at this question once more.

▶ *Fee income generated by a handful of early franchisees should never be the main attraction. What should prompt you to franchise your business is the concept's potential to grow your network more rapidly than would otherwise be possible.*

▶ *As soon as the network reaches critical mass, usually around 25 to 50 units, income from franchise fees becomes highly attractive. At the same time, various economies of scale will begin to kick in, for example in product sourcing and national advertising. From this point onwards, the sky is truly the limit.*

Franchise fees under the spotlight

I have already mentioned several types of payments franchisees are expected to make. I will now explain how these fees are usually calculated and what they are intended to pay for.

THE INITIAL FRANCHISE FEE

This fee is usually payable by the franchisee to the franchisor upon signing the franchise contract. It is a once-off lump sum, sometimes also described as a 'joining fee'. Paying it entitles the franchisee to join the network and receive initial training and assistance with the establishment of the business. It also gives the franchisee access to the network's intellectual property. In this context, 'intellectual property' refers to the network's trademark plus the franchisor's trade contacts and operating expertise.

Calculating the initial fee

Although no binding rule for calculating the initial franchise fee exists, experienced franchise professionals have come up with a formula that is widely used for this purpose:

> **Projected establishment costs + mark-up ÷ number of franchisees expected to join during the initial 3–5 years after the launch = initial fee**

PROJECTED ESTABLISHMENT COSTS

This is the sum total of expenses the franchisor expects to incur during the establishment phase, say the initial three to five years. These costs include development costs, professional fees, franchise marketing costs, franchisee recruitment and selection costs and the costs incurred in easing the new franchisee into his or her business.

MARK-UP

In this context, mark-up refers to the amount you add to the projected establishment costs as profit. During the early stages, when the network's goodwill is limited, this figure will be relatively low. It can be increased over time as the 'pulling power' of the brand increases. The paragraph below headed 'Additional thoughts on initial fees' explores this topic further.

NUMBER OF FRANCHISEES
The franchisor will wish to recoup the costs incurred in creating the initial franchise package as quickly as possible. This is understandable but you need to be careful to avoid penalizing early joiners by expecting them to shoulder the full burden. In other words, the total amount you expect to spend on setting up the franchise operation needs to be spread over a realistic number of franchisees. 'What is a realistic number of franchisees?' I hear you ask. I would define it as the number of franchisees you expect to join your growing network within the initial three to five years after launch.

Additional thoughts on initial fees
Most franchise experts agree that the initial franchise fee should be set relatively low, for several reasons.

▶ *The initial fee falls due at a time when the new franchisee sees vast amounts of his or her money going out but nothing coming in. This is bound to create anxiety at the precise point wjhen a positive mindset is essential.*
▶ *Some banks may be reluctant to finance the initial franchise fee portion of the total investment. The reason for this is that the initial fee does not pay for a tangible asset. Should the fee be set too high, this could put the opportunity out of reach of candidates that might otherwise be an asset to the network. This could impact negatively on sustained growth.*
▶ *Franchising is not about selling 'rights to territories'. The rationale for the establishment of a business under franchise should be the creation of realistic and sustainable business ventures. The focus of the business should always be on the sale of a product or service for which demand exists.*
    ▷ *The franchisor should derive its income primarily from management services fees. Subject to circumstances, but*

*always as a secondary consideration, income from the
supply of products might come into the equation.*

▷ *The franchisee should profit from the sale of the
network's products or services.*

▶ *Initial fees should be in line with those charged by direct
competitors. Should this be unrealistic then the franchisor
should at least be able to justify the difference, for example by
pointing to the superior initial support the network offers.*

Case study 1

An entrepreneur has this great idea for the establishment
of a chain of restaurants. He has a degree in business, is an
excellent chef and the first unit he has set up is a resounding
success. The business is new, however, and the entrepreneur
does not have sufficient money to finance the development of
a proper franchise package. He decides to raise the necessary
capital by selling franchises. He does not know anything about
franchising, however, and asks you to advise him. What would
your comment be and why?

ESTABLISHMENT COSTS

In addition to paying the upfront fee to the franchisor, a new
franchisee needs to pay for the equipment, vehicles, fittings and
furnishings, or whatever else is needed to set up the business. He
or she is also responsible for the cost of purchasing initial stock
and any other items required to get the business ready for trading.
Depending on network policy, the franchisor may:

▶ *Act as the supplier of some of the items needed to set up the
business.*

▶ *Supply a turnkey operation. (A turnkey operation is a business
that has been set up and fully equipped by the franchisor. The*

moment it is handed over to the franchisee, the franchisee can start trading.)

▶ *Hand the franchisee a list of items to be purchased, usually from prescribed sources.*

Regardless of the way this issue is dealt with, three things should be in place:

▶ *The franchisor should have tested the prescribed items in its own unit to ensure that they are fit for their intended purpose.*
▶ *The cost to the franchisee should be at least as favourable, preferably lower than if he or she would source items of comparable quality on the open market.*
▶ *The franchisee has been told upfront that he or she is responsible for payment. A reasonable estimate of the amount the franchisee will require to fund the establishment of the business should be provided as early as possible during the negotiations, certainly before the franchise agreement is signed.*

Insight

In the interest of maintaining a relationship of trust, franchise practitioners recommend that should the franchisor obtain financial incentives in exchange for naming nominated suppliers, this fact should be disclosed to the prospective franchisee upfront. Most national franchise associations around the globe make this binding on their members.

WORKING CAPITAL

The franchisee needs to fund working capital requirements. Working capital is the amount of cash the franchisee needs to pay ongoing costs linked to the operation of the business until it becomes self-funding. Depending on the nature and size of the business, this amount tends to vary considerably from one franchise opportunity to the next.

In a business-to-business environment, for example, it is usually necessary to keep significant amounts of goods in stock and offer customers extended payment terms. Both these realities can weigh heavily on cash flow. In a fast-food place, on the other hand, the value of stock will be low and practically all sales are for cash.

All these aspects need to be taken into consideration.

TOTAL COST OF ESTABLISHING A FRANCHISE

How much should you expect to invest in a franchise opportunity? It would be meaningless to state a specific amount because the extent of your investment depends on many factors, including the industry sector you wish to invest in and the nature and size of the business. As a rough guide, I can tell you that current levels of total investment range from £7 000 to £1 000 000 and over.

Within the franchise environment, banks are generally willing to provide loans for between 50 and 70 per cent of the total amount required. You will read more about this under the heading 'Securing finance for a franchise' later in this chapter.

ONGOING FRANCHISE FEES

Almost without exception, franchisees are obliged to pay ongoing fees to the franchisor. The major types of fees are the management services fee and the contribution to the network's management fund.

Management services fee

It is good practice that every franchisor should levy a management services fee. Even if the franchisor expects to be the main supplier of goods for resale to its franchisees and may be content to earn a mark-up on these goods, a management services fee should be charged. As the franchisor's obligations extend well beyond those of a supplier, it is better to treat the supply of products and the provision of ongoing support services to franchisees as separate issues.

The income the franchisor derives from management services fees should pay for the operation of the franchisee support infrastructure and allow a fair profit. Ideally, the management services fee should be the franchisor's main source of income. This is in the interest of franchisees because it provides an incentive for the franchisor to offer extensive ongoing support.

VARIABLE MANAGEMENT SERVICES FEE

It is customary to calculate the management services fee (MSF) as a percentage of the franchisee's sales or purchases. This fee is payable by the franchisee to the franchisor in weekly or monthly intervals as stipulated in the franchise agreement.

Most experts agree that this is the fairest way of calculating the franchise fee. Problems can arise if franchisees are extremely successful; once they exceed certain sales levels, they feel that they are being penalized for doing a good job.

Some franchisors try to address this by staggering fee percentages. For example, MSF might be set at 7 per cent for the first £100 000 sales per month, dropping to 4 per cent beyond that. This can create problems of its own, for example if the franchisor is the main supplier of products for resale and is unable to deliver full order quantities. The franchisee will claim that he would have exceeded target and is therefore entitled to pay the lower rate.

Tip

In my experience, it is better to charge a uniform percentage level but reinvest more into successful franchisees' businesses. This can be done, for example, in the form of additional training and marketing support.

FIXED MANAGEMENT SERVICES FEE

Some franchisors levy a fixed fee. This means that the franchisee is compelled to pay a fixed amount regardless of sales levels. Some franchisors justify their decision to levy a fixed fee by claiming that far too many franchisees are inherently dishonest. Should they rely on fee income based on a percentage of sales, these franchisees would under-declare sales to reduce fee payments.

This argument ignores the fact that franchisors have a moral obligation and usually the contractual right to monitor their franchisees' business performance. This should enable them to gauge the fidelity of franchisees' fee returns. If it is impractical to monitor franchisees' business performance, the business might not be franchiseable. An example would be the provider of a service that does not use measurable supplies. In such an instance, another avenue for business expansion might be more appropriate.

At this point, I must stress that some very ethical franchisors levy fixed management services fees. In most instances, these franchisors supply a product to their franchisees and are content to make their money in the form of a mark-up on product sales. Feedback from their franchisees suggests that they are extremely happy with the deal. But while this simplifies controls and may suit some franchisees, it is also open to abuse. By charging a fixed amount, the franchisor may be tempted to remove the all-important risk/reward scenario from the equation. I say 'may' advisedly because quite clearly, if the franchisor is the supplier of a product, the incentive to support its franchisees even if they pay a fixed fee remains.

Should the franchisor not benefit from product supplies, however, it could decide to focus on selling additional territories rather than support established franchisees. Although this would not be sustainable, it would provide the franchisor with a series of windfalls in the form of upfront fees followed by a fixed monthly income, albeit for a limited period. This period would end as soon as the hapless franchisee calls it quits. And should the franchisee manage to soldier on for the duration of the agreement, he or she would be unlikely to renew it once it expires.

A fixed fee arrangement has drawbacks for the franchisor as well. Fees are fixed for the duration of the franchise agreement. Should the fee be set too high, franchisees may not be able to survive the initial two to three years when sales have to build up. If, on the other hand, the fee is set too low, franchisors will not be able to profit from the ongoing support they offer their franchisees once these franchisees' sales have reached worthwhile levels.

Setting management services fee levels

Typical fee levels for MSF range from 3 per cent to 10 per cent of sales. That's a wide range but, looked upon in isolation, the percentage figure is generally meaningless. To assess fee levels realistically, you need to investigate the nature of the business, the sales levels you can expect to achieve, attainable margins and the extent of the franchisor's support infrastructure.

▶ *In sectors that trade in a high sales volume/low margin environment, for example the bulk retailing of groceries, the percentage figure could be as low as 0.5 to 1 per cent.*
   ▷ *This keeps the fee affordable for franchisees.*
   ▷ *The high sales volumes that are typically achieved in this environment will ensure that the franchisor's fee income remains attractive.*
▶ *Should sales volumes be relatively low but mark-ups high, as is often the case in simple service operations like home repairs or cleaning, a much higher percentage needs to be levied as franchise fee. This ensures the franchisor an adequate income, and the franchisee can easily afford it.*

▶ *The franchise fee must be affordable and each franchisee should receive the same deal;*
▶ *Franchisees should have the distinct feeling that they receive value for their money in the form of ongoing support;*

▶ *Fee income must allow the franchisor to make a profit.*
▶ *Unless all these factors are in place, the network is unlikely to prosper.*

Royalty payments

On occasion, the management services fee (MSF) is described as a royalty but this could give rise to misunderstandings. Royalty income is generally understood to be passive income, the person or company that is entitled to receive royalties is not expected to provide ongoing services. An example would be a singer who records a chart-topping song. He or she will receive royalties based on sales without having to do anything other than sing the song in the recording studio.

This contrasts sharply with the franchisor's obligations. In return for receiving ongoing fees from members of the network, the franchisor is expected to provide extensive ongoing support to franchisees. The difference is significant and goes well beyond mere semantics.

Of course, in addition to receiving ongoing support from their franchisor, franchisees are also entitled to use the network's trademark and other intellectual property. One could argue, therefore, that the MSF contains a royalty element but this would complicate matters unnecessarily.

Case study 2

You are talking to two different franchisors in the same business sector. The one levies a MSF of 7 per cent based on sales while the other is content to receive 5 per cent.

Which franchisor offers the better deal and why?

CASE STUDY

The marketing services fund

Most franchise networks operate a marketing fund or similar vehicle. It is funded jointly by the network's members and pays for brand building and product advertising. In addition to all franchisees in the network, the franchisor's own units should contribute to this fund as they stand to benefit from the resulting marketing activities.

Many franchisors calculate contributions to the marketing fund as a percentage of sales. Once again, percentage figures vary, but expect them to range between 1 and 4 per cent of sales. Alternatively, the franchisor might charge a fixed fee. In this instance, charging a fixed fee may be justified because it facilitates budgeting. Because the marketing services fund receives a predictable income stream throughout the year, campaigns can be planned better. This will enhance their effectiveness and enables the network to negotiate better deals.

Although the marketing fund is usually administered at head office level, forward-looking franchisors will grant franchisees a voice in deciding how the fund's monies are to be spent. This is usually done through a franchisee representative committee, marketing committee or similar structure. You will read more about this in Chapter 6.

SUNDRY FINANCIAL OBLIGATIONS

Local advertising

Some networks compel their franchisees to spend a predetermined amount of money on local advertising campaigns. This would be in addition to the contributions they make to the network's marketing fund. The rationale is that while the marketing fund pays for regional or national campaigns, franchisees need to maximize their effectiveness by plugging into them at local level.

Additional franchisor services

In addition to the standard range of franchisee support services
provided by franchisors worthy of that name, some networks
offer their franchisees additional services. An example would be
a comprehensive administration service. As this would obviate
the need for individual franchisees to establish an administration
infrastructure at unit level, it has the potential to reduce costs.
As store administration is the responsibility of each franchisee,
however, the franchisor would be entitled to recoup its costs. This
is acceptable as long as franchisees obtain genuine bulk benefits.

Please take note

Good franchise practice suggests that if a franchisor intends
to make local advertising or additional franchisor services
compulsory, this should be subject to the following provisos:

▶ *Prospective franchisees should be informed of these additional
financial obligations as early as possible during negotiations,
certainly long before it comes to the signing of the franchise
agreement.*
▶ *The imposition of additional financial obligations upon
existing franchisees should only be considered if the vast
majority agree that this benefits them.*

Compulsory purchases

Many companies become franchisors because they want to set up
a network of captive outlets for their product range and there is
nothing wrong with that. From the franchisee's point of view, bulk
purchase arrangements often rate among the main attractions for
joining a franchise. Provided that such an arrangement is handled
ethically, it will benefit both parties. Possible scenarios are:

▶ *The franchisor is the manufacturer, importer or bulk
distributor of a product. This product is distributed through
the franchised network, either exclusively or the network's
franchisees receive preferential deals.*

► *The franchisor negotiates with the network's suppliers and arranges preferential pricing based on network-wide projected volumes. Franchisees deal directly with the supplier but qualify for the negotiated (lower) price.*

  ▷ *In the interest of consistency throughout the network and to achieve negotiated volumes, the franchisor is likely to compel franchisees to purchase exclusively from approved suppliers.*

  ▷ *The arrangement should be subject to franchisees deriving a clear benefit from the arrangement. Should this benefit cease to exist, the franchisor would have a moral obligation to renegotiate on behalf of the network.*

  ▷ *Should the franchisor receive some financial incentive from approved suppliers to the network, ethics demand that franchisees should be made aware of this.*

Provision for periodic refurbishing

To keep abreast of the competition in a rapidly changing market place, franchised networks are forced to maintain a fresh look. This means that the appearance of their stores needs to be changed from time to time and/or equipment used in the units needs to be updated.

To ensure that this happens, franchisees are compelled to undertake upgrades at specified intervals, usually five to seven years after commencement of operations. This could involve a major capital outlay and needs to be considered when viability studies are made.

Renewal fee

Franchise agreements are long-term agreements, valid for between five and seven years but this period can be up to 20 years. In view of the substantial investment franchisees are compelled to make, it is customary to offer them an option to extend the agreement for a further period. Renewal is usually conditional upon the franchisee accepting the terms contained in the franchise agreement offered to new franchisees at the time the renewal occurs.

There is an emerging trend to charge a further fixed fee when the contract comes up for renewal. This fee is usually equal to the initial fee in force at the time of renewal. This trend originated in the United States where franchisors justify their stance by claiming that due to the aggressive marketing campaigns they conduct, the pulling power of the brand has increased. As this will impact positively on the franchisee's future sales, he or she stands to benefit directly and must pay.

Critics of the practice point out that over the lifespan of the initial contract, the franchisee has made a significant contribution towards the growth of the brand. In addition to putting up the original investment, the franchisee has worked in the unit and made regular payments in the form of franchise fees. Charging the franchisee a renewal fee would amount to double-dipping.

Insight

Currently, renewal fees are a moot point the world over and no binding guidelines exist. If faced by this demand, you have to assess it on its merits. If the brand is worth it, why quibble?

Securing finance for a franchise

No matter what business model you finally select, raising the necessary finance is usually a major concern. The good news is that prospective franchisees enjoy a head start. Bankers know that franchisees of a reputable franchisor stand a much better chance of long-term success than independents. The same does not necessarily apply to the prospective franchisor – at the start-up stage, a project to expand an existing business through franchising will be evaluated just like any other expansion plan. However, programmes to assist prospective franchisees and prospective franchisors are in place and I will deal with them later in this chapter.

GENERAL CONSIDERATIONS

To establish a franchise network or to purchase a franchise requires a significant investment. Unless the new venture can be financed entirely from available cash resources, you will need to approach your bank for a loan or find another source of capital. But although investment capital is readily available, the problem is that new entrepreneurs are often unfamiliar with the various options available to them. Should you find yourself in this situation, it could lock you into the wrong type of funding structure at best. At worst, it could sink your plans.

You need to understand that raising finance isn't just about asking the banker for a certain amount of money and crossing your fingers that he or she will agree. To enhance your chances for success, your approach needs to be a little more sophisticated than that. Before you ask a banker for a loan, you need to formulate credible answers to the following five questions:

1 *How much money do I need and by when do I need it?*
2 *What exactly do I need the money for?*
3 *What type of finance is best suited for this purpose?*
4 *How do I propose to repay the money?*
5 *Is it worth the risk?*

To create the desired response, answers to these questions must be based on fact and compiling them will be hard work. You will have to draw up a comprehensive business plan and financial projections. Should you be a little unsure about the process, don't worry. Guidelines are given in Appendix 1, and major banks provide templates on their websites.

At this stage, you will not be able to formulate accurate answers to many of the questions I pose. You will only be ready for that once you have identified a specific franchise offer and have received a set of figures reflecting financial performance. I consider it useful, however, to get you thinking about finance-related issues as early as possible. Once you understand how it all fits together and have put a basic framework in place, slotting in actual figures will be quick and easy.

> **Tip**
>
> If you ask the bank you plan to approach for a loan to give you a business plan template early on, you will have plenty of time to familiarize yourself with it. Using the bank's template has the added advantage that the banker will be comfortable with the layout you use.

1 How much money do I need and by when do I need it?

Being ambitious can be a good thing but you need to be realistic here. Don't waste your time planning a project of such magnitude that you have no realistic chance of securing the required funding. Not only will the experience of being rejected demoralize you, it may also close doors to other useful contacts. It is much better to aim for an investment in the range you know you can support. When you work out how much money you will need you should to consider the following:

▶ *Over-funding: No matter how you look at it, money will cost you money. I am referring here to the possibility that you allocate more funds to the new business project than you actually need. This would cost you dearly, either in extra interest you have to pay if you borrow the money, or in lost opportunity cost if you keep the money accessible because you could invest it elsewhere.*

▶ *Under-funding: Asking for too little money upfront would be an even greater mistake. You would risk running out of cash before the new business had a chance to prove its viability, and this could seriously derail you. If you don't need all the money at once, ask for the full amount but request permission to make draw-downs in certain intervals. This way, you won't pay interest on money you don't immediately need.*

Tip

When you work out the total investment amount, keep in mind that you need to make a reasonable contribution from your own cash resources. As a rule of thumb, bankers will lend a prospective franchisee of a credible network between 50 and 70 per cent of the total. This is subject to your track record and the availability of adequate security. It also means that if you can contribute, say, £20 000 in ready cash, you should look at investments in the £40 000 to £65 000 bracket.

2 What exactly do I need the money for?

You can't just waltz into a banker's office, ask for an amount of money 'to start a business' and expect him or her to write out a cheque. As part of your business plan, you will need to prepare a detailed schedule of items you need to purchase at the start-up stage, and state the approximate cost of each.

If you are short of surety, it is best to stick to items that are widely in use. The banker might be able to accept them as partial security for the loan. Experience suggests that it is far more difficult to obtain finance for highly specialized machinery than for standard equipment because if you fail, the banker will find it more difficult to resell the former.

3 What type of finance is best suited for this purpose?

Should you be a newcomer to the business world, you might be surprised to learn that loans come in different flavours. To impress your banker by showing him or her that you know what you are talking about you need to be familiar with the different types of finance that are available and their intended purpose. It also means that you should be able to explain how you plan to fund your business (the funding mix). The different types of finance that are most commonly used in the small business environment are detailed below.

EQUITY FINANCE

1 Own cash resources

Your ability to invest some money of your own into the venture is a fundamental requirement. This is only fair and reasonable – you cannot expect a financier to invest in your business unless you are willing and able to do the same. In any event, borrowing 100 per cent of the required funds would put tremendous strain on your business's cash flow.

This is always an issue but even more so during the initial stages when your business is an unproven entity. Those suppliers who grant you credit are likely to watch your payment performance like hawks. Should you be late with even one payment, they are likely to freeze your account. This could put the survival of your business at risk.

2 Soft loans

Loans by family and friends are also known as soft loans because they are usually unsecured, no fixed repayment period has been set and they may even be interest-free. A soft loan is usually not reflected on the business's balance sheet – the money is loaned to you in your personal capacity and you invest it in the business as if it were your own.

As a result, the person who lends you the money would have no claim against the business. Should the business fail, his or her chances of recouping the full amount would be slim to non-existent. This form of loan is also known as 'off-balance sheet financing'. Many business start-ups have been financed in this way and have grown to a size where traditional forms of finance could be tapped. But negative experiences are on record as well.

On occasion, a sound business has to be closed down because of the way a soft loan has been structured. What usually happens is that either the investor demands a disproportionate amount of influence over the way the business should be run, or internal quarrels prompt him or her to ask for repayment of the full amount. Should this request come at a stage in the business's development when its cash flow is weak, the business could run out of cash and fail.

A formal loan agreement between the lender and yourself, drafted by a solicitor with expertise in such matters, should reflect the terms of the loan as well as the respective rights and obligations of lender and borrower. This reduces the risk of problems occurring at a later stage and is well worth the solicitor's fee.

3 Investment by co-owners
You can raise funds by taking on business partners. In return for making an investment and/or bringing in needed skills, the new entrant would become the owner of a portion of the business. In addition to making an investment, he or she will become jointly and severally liable for the financial obligations of the business and will be entitled to a share of the profits in return.

In a small business context, a partnership works best if the partner injects some expertise into the business that has been lacking in the past. If, for example, you are technically minded, you might benefit most if you attract a partner with expertise in accounting or marketing.

Insight

Funds that have been invested in the business are known as equity finance. Those who invest it become part owners of the business on a pro-rata basis and cannot simply withdraw the money – it belongs to the business. Should an investor wish to withdraw his or her funds, they must offer their share of the business for sale. To prevent problems arising at this point, co-owners of the business should enter into a formal agreement that stipulates how the withdrawal of a part owner will be handled.

BANK FINANCE
As long as you as the owner of the business are able to provide a reasonable portion of the capital from your own resources, a possible shortfall can be funded through a loan provided by a commercial lender, usually a bank. Loans come in several forms, each with its own advantages and disadvantages. It is important that you choose the right type of loan for your needs. Your accountant and, at a later stage, your franchisor, will no doubt advise. You will be more comfortable, however, if you know what they are talking about.

1 Overdraft

An overdraft is the most common form of loan finance in the small business environment. Not only is it the easiest to obtain, if used correctly, it is also the cheapest. Once you have applied, and as soon as the bank has advised you of the set overdraft limit, you will be able to draw on your bank account, up to the agreed limit, just as if you had the money in the bank. The bank will charge you interest on the actual debit balance. If, on certain days of the month, your account is in credit, you are not using your overdraft and no debit interest will be payable.

Overdrafts are intended as bridging finance, to help you over parts of the month when your business's cash flow is under strain. The bank's expectation is that your account shows a credit balance at least some of the time. You need to be aware that an overdraft is granted 'on call'. In other words, your bank could call up the outstanding balance at any time, and without giving any reasons.

Don't think for a moment that if you keep your financial affairs in order, this will never happen. It can happen for a variety of reasons, some entirely beyond your control. If and when it does, it can have a devastating effect on the financial affairs of your business. For this reason, overdraft finance must never be used to finance major investments of a long-term nature.

2 Fixed rate loans

If you need a loan to purchase equipment or other fixed assets, a fixed rate loan might be the best choice. Such loans are granted for periods of between 12 and 120 months. They are repayable in monthly instalments to which interest at a fixed rate will be added. Before a loan application is approved, the bank will expect you to present a loan proposal that is backed by a detailed business plan.

On approval of your application, the bank will enter into a written loan agreement with you that will reflect the agreed terms and conditions for the loan. Study it carefully before you sign it, then file your copy away in a safe place.

For as long as you adhere to the agreed repayment schedule, your bank is unlikely to call up the entire outstanding balance of the loan prematurely. However, the bank will protect its interests by inserting a clause into the loan agreement to the effect that should the bank become aware of adverse circumstances surrounding your business it may recall the outstanding balance at once. Should you fall behind with payments without discussing this with your banker beforehand then the bank will almost certainly invoke this clause.

Subject to the terms of the agreement you have reached with your bank, loan capital can be used to finance the purchase of equipment, office furniture and initial stock, or even to bolster working capital reserves. Interest rates are lower than those charged for an overdraft but interest remains payable even if your current account shows a credit balance.

3 Base rate loans
A base rate loan is linked to the base rate; in other words, interest tends to fluctuate. Base rate loans are granted for periods between 12 and 240 months and provide some flexibility. For example, recognizing that cash flow is likely to be under pressure during the start-up period, the bank may agree to grant you a repayment holiday of up to two years. This means that for this initial period, you would service interest only. Capital repayments would be spread over the balance of the agreed loan period.

4 Treasury fixed rate loans
To fund a franchise in the higher investment bracket may require you to take out a treasury fixed rate loan. The loan period can be up to 25 years, and repayment can be structured to suit the business's cash flow patterns. The minimum loan amount is usually £100 000 and in addition to interest, an arrangement fee is payable. As the interest is calculated upfront for the full term of the loan, you will be penalized should you wish to repay the loan early.

5 Factoring

Businesses that supply other businesses on credit terms and have substantial turnovers can free up their cash flow, at a price, by 'selling' their debtors' book to a discounter, for example a bank. Depending on the assessed quality of the debtors' book, the discounter will advance a percentage of outstanding amounts upfront and pay the balance upon receiving payments from debtors; finance charges will usually be deducted from the final amount.

This form of finance is relatively expensive but it enables rapidly growing businesses to grasp opportunities as they present themselves without facing the risk of running out of working capital.

6 Business charge cards

Charge cards are a convenient payment mechanism and also offer free credit over a limited period. If administered correctly, they provide better control over spending.

7 Other forms of finance

Depending on your specific circumstances, your bank may offer you finance for the purchase of business vehicles and premises. Vehicles are usually financed through a hire purchase arrangement. Should you wish to purchase your own business premises, a commercial mortgage is the most likely option. It is best to discuss your needs with your banker well before you actually need the cash. Firstly, you will be able to enter into favourable deals because in the vendor's eyes, you qualify as a cash buyer. And seeing that you are not under time pressure, you will be able to shop around for the best finance charges as well.

DEALING WITH COMMERCIAL BANKS

A certain mystique has surrounded banking for centuries and some of it has managed to survive to this day. Considering that we live in a time when old bastions of authority have crumbled and cynicism is the order of the day, this is rather surprising but remains a fact nonetheless. Many people continue to see bankers as creatures with almost supernatural powers, in a position of authority that allows them to decide the fate of a small business at a whim. To them, bankers are the custodians of piles of cash that they will lend only to a select group, with the decision to grant a loan being based solely on long-established affiliations and personal preferences.

In the real world, banking is nothing of this sort. In a banker's hands, cash is practically the same as the merchandise a retailer offers for sale. Bankers accept money from depositors who expect to receive interest. They in turn lend this money out to borrowers whom they charge interest, obviously at a higher level. The differential between the two interest rates enables bankers to generate profits for their shareholders.

I admit that this may be an oversimplification of the way banking works, but it illustrates the point that bankers are practically forced to lend out money. Would they fail to do that and keep the money safely in their vaults instead, they would soon go out of business. However, the banker's desire to lend out money is counterbalanced by his or her obligation to ensure that the money is paid back within the agreed period, and with interest.

The traditional way of protecting the bank against losses arising from bad debt has been to have loans secured by assets that exceed the value of the outstanding loan and can easily be realized. It follows that unless you were able to tap informal sources of finance, your request for a loan would have been met with a request to provide security or collateral.

Although the banks' advertising may suggest otherwise, this has not changed very much. Security remains an issue, but there is light at the end nonetheless. As long as an entrepreneur has a sound business plan and a realistic approach towards business, he or she will at least get a hearing. While in the past, bankers perceived hard assets such as blue chip investments and fixed property as the only acceptable form of collateral, forward-looking bankers are prepared to assess the entrepreneur's potential. Moreover, they consider the promise

contained in a sound business plan as a form of collateral – for part
of the loan at least. And better things are yet to come!

Important note

It pays to talk to the experts. Should you visit a branch of one
of the major commercial banks yet come face to face with a
banker who appears less than enthusiastic about franchising,
insist on being referred to the dedicated franchise division
of the bank if they have one. Four leading banks in the UK
have specialists on their staff whose sole job it is to promote
franchise finance. Seek them out, talk to them and you may
well find that they can offer you much more than just money.
They can be an invaluable source of useful advice in various
areas ranging from franchise expertise to what type of finance
would meet your needs best.

Small firms loan guarantee

Governments the world over are keen to promote small business
and the UK is no exception. The Department for Business
Innovation and Skills (BIS) offers loan guarantees designed to make
loan applications bankable even though the applicant may not have
sufficient collateral. In other countries, this function is typically the
responsibility of the Department of Trade and Industry (DTI) or
similar organization. This is how it usually works:

▶ *Applications for loan guarantees must be channelled through
registered commercial lenders, usually your bank. The bank
has the right to approve or reject your loan application.
Should the bank agree that your project appears to be sound
but he or she cannot grant the loan because you cannot offer
sufficient security, the BIS guarantee comes into play. (In other
countries, it will be the DTI.)*
▶ *Your loan application will be forwarded to the BIS. The BIS
assesses each application on its merit and will usually approve
or reject it within five working days. If granted, this guarantee
adds an extra 2 per cent per annum to the interest charge.*
▶ *The BIS indemnifies the bank up to a maximum of 75 per cent
of the outstanding loan amount. This means that should you
default on repayments, the BIS will pay the bank the bulk of*

the outstanding amount but you are not off the hook. The bank is obliged to do everything reasonably possible to recoup the outstanding balance from you before claiming from the BIS. Should the bank manage to collect from you after the BIS has settled the claim, it must reimburse the BIS.

4 How do I propose to repay the money?

The next thing the banker will want to know is how you plan to repay the loan. This means that you have to project sales, profitability and cash flows over the entire life of the loan. What the banker will be most interested in is the business's ability to generate the cash needed to pay off the loan plus interest. In this context, you need to remember that to be sustainable, loan repayments have to be made from operating profits.

Begin drafting your financial projections by forecasting expected levels of sales and profitability. Base these figures on realistic assumptions and explain why you think that they are attainable. Bankers like to see records of past performance but this being a start-up you will have to base your projections on the financial performance of comparable established units within the network. The banker is likely to accept that, as long as you take the demographics of the proposed site and competitor activity in the neighbourhood into account.

Once you have completed the original set of financial projections, you need to prepare two variants. For want of a better title, head them 'better than expected scenario' and 'worse than expected scenario'.

▶ *Should sales be significantly higher than expected, you will need to purchase more goods, perhaps hire additional staff and your debtors' book will swell. This may put pressure on your working capital reserves.*
▶ *If the worst-case scenario materializes, the banker will want to see how you plan to cope with that. Ideally, you should be able to list some fixed asset that can be readily turned into cash.*

You can really only deal with these issues once you have access to the financial projections for the franchise you plan to join but, as I said before, it is a good thing to start thinking about them early on.

5 Is it worth the risk?

I stated in an earlier chapter that the thought of making plenty of money should not be the sole motivator for going into business. However, the opposite holds true as well. Starting a business of your own is an exciting prospect, and for a while, you might think that this in itself is sufficient reward. It is hard work, however, and unless your efforts generate reasonable financial rewards, you will eventually grow tired of the endless slog. This is only human, and your banker knows that. So, if your financial projections predict marginal profits at best, he or she will be reluctant to fund the venture.

FRANCHISE-FRIENDLY BANKS

Given franchising's proud history it is not surprising that bankers generally have a sound grasp of the concept and embrace it with gusto. The reason for their enthusiasm is not hard to find. Instead of being exposed to the ramblings of a wild-eyed entrepreneur who has neither a track record to speak of nor any proof that his business idea will work, the banker is presented with a professionally prepared loan proposal which is underpinned by the reputation of the franchisor. Although a franchisor is unlikely to guarantee the loan, the mere fact that the applicant has been accepted as a franchisee gives the banker some comfort.

Selecting a bank

On the surface of it, all banks may appear to be the same – similar advertising – similar approach to lending – similar range of products – similar level of service. In the case of franchise finance, this isn't always fair. Although all major banks are familiar with franchising, I believe that not all of them go the proverbial extra mile in an attempt to maximize lending to this sector. However, several leading banks do so – you can identify them through their involvement in franchise-related promotional events like exhibitions and seminars. This notwithstanding, banks' policies tend to change over time and 'shopping around' is always a good idea.

What your bank should do for you

Ideally, your bank should operate a dedicated programme for the franchise sector. To begin with, this means that the bank has franchise expertise on tap, not just at head office level but throughout the regions, so that you can access it conveniently in your area. This is important, especially if you are a prospective franchisee and require guidance on how you should go about financing your franchise.

Turning to the bank's product offering, a specific programme should be in place for franchisors and their franchisees, in that order. Starting at the foundations, such a programme would revolve around close cooperation between the bank and carefully selected franchisors. To be admitted, franchisors would have to provide the bank with comprehensive information on their franchise package and details of their franchisee support infrastructure.

Having satisfied itself of a franchisor's bona fides including its performance record, the fairness of the franchise agreement, the extent of initial and ongoing franchisee support and the financial viability of the franchise, the bank would ideally enter into a formal cooperation agreement with the franchisor. To be meaningful, such an arrangement would offer a series of benefits to the franchisor as well as to prospective and existing franchisees of the network.

To be considered 'franchise friendly' a bank should ideally offer the following services:

- ▶ *Initial and ongoing access to franchise information;*
- ▶ *Computerized business plan layouts and cash flow models;*
- ▶ *Creative financing solutions which, in appropriate circumstances, should include an initial loan repayment holiday;*
- ▶ *Dedicated banking products, made available to qualifying franchisors and their franchisees at preferential rates;*

- ▶ *A comprehensive range of traditional and electronic banking facilities including credit card merchant services, permitting true and literal one-stop banking;*
- ▶ *Ongoing close cooperation between franchisor, franchisees and the bank's relationship manager, with the objective of fostering a climate of cooperation and fiscal responsibility;*
- ▶ *Joint implementation of an intensive care programme designed to minimize the risk of struggling franchisees actually failing.*

Reality check

Even the most forward-thinking banker is unlikely to approve a loan application unless you are able to top up the loan amount with a reasonable contribution from your own resources. Your contribution should preferably be in cash, as the mere fact that you have accumulated some capital indicates your ability to deal with financial matters in a responsible manner. Other reasons for this requirement are:

- ▶ *If loan capital is the only source of finance, interest charges and repayments are likely to absorb all the business's profits and strangle its cash flow.*
- ▶ *Unless you have a tangible investment in the business, your commitment to the project might be suspect. Should the going get tough for a while, and you having nothing to lose, you could easily decide to lock up the business, hand the banker the keys and walk away.*

RAISING FINANCE – PROSPECTIVE FRANCHISEE

Bankers acknowledge that franchisees of reputable networks have a much better chance to become successful than entrepreneurs who try to develop an unproven concept and have to fend for themselves. I have seen statistics that place the survival rate of franchisees as high as 90 per cent and that of their independent counterparts as low as 10 per cent. As these and similar figures are difficult to verify, I do not wish to dwell on them too much. Let us just agree that when you want to start a business, franchising is the safer option.

Bankers are extremely keen to offer finance to prospective franchisees, on occasion as much as 50 to 70 per cent of the total capital required. After all, far from being an untested start-up, the new venture will operate under the name of the franchise network, using its proven techniques and enjoying ongoing support by a team of seasoned professionals. This goes a long way towards reassuring the banker.

Add to this possible access to the small firms loan guarantee, explained earlier in this chapter, and suddenly even loan proposals that may have been considered unsound by yesteryear's bankers become bankable. This is obviously subject to your creditworthiness and, as they say, conditions apply. What I am really saying here is that even if you appear to meet all the requirements I have listed, there is no guarantee that your loan proposal will be approved. Let me reiterate, however, that if you select a reputable franchisor, present your banker with a viable business plan and your background checks out, you stand an excellent chance of obtaining the funding you need.

In this case, as in so many others, the secret is to go into battle well prepared. The following table contains some of the questions a banker will probably want you to answer.

Questions a banker is likely to ask prospective franchisees

Personal details

- ▶ *What is your full name, address?*
- ▶ *What is your age and marital status?*
- ▶ *Any children? If so, their ages?*
- ▶ *What is the status of your health?*
- ▶ *Do you have any physical handicaps? (This question needs to be asked because an individual suffering from vertigo, for*

example, could not function very well as a franchisee of a roof repair company.)

▶ *What is the level of your formal education and when did you complete it?*
▶ *What courses have you attended since?*
▶ *Did you participate in any formal or informal work-related training?*
▶ *What is your past work experience?*
▶ *What are your personal interests?*
▶ *What are your plans for the future?*

Employment/business details

▶ *What work do you currently do?*
▶ *Do you have a history of operating in a small business environment?*
▶ *Which business sector are you interested in and why?*
▶ *Do you have any hands-on experience in this sector?*
▶ *Where is the sector headed and how do you know?*
▶ *Which brands are seen as the market leaders in this sector and why?*
▶ *Do you fully understand how franchising works?*
▶ *Are you prepared to live with the restrictions the franchisor may impose on your freedom to act?*

Franchise details

▶ *Which brand are you interested in and why?*
▶ *Have you spoken to the franchisor and do they have a suitable territory available?*
▶ *What do you know about this particular opportunity?*
▶ *Have you received financial projections and a copy of the franchise agreement?*
▶ *Have you spoken to existing franchisees?*
▶ *Did you work in a company-owned store to see what it's like?*

▶ *Did you receive financial projections and a copy of the franchise agreement? If so, did you have your professional advisers check these out?*

Financial issues

▶ *What is your current income?*
▶ *What is your net worth (assets less liabilities – provide an up-to-date balance sheet)?*
▶ *What assets can you offer as surety for a loan and how much equity do you have in them?*
▶ *What is your credit history and can you name some credit references?*
▶ *How much money do you plan to borrow?*
▶ *What type of loan would you prefer and why?*
▶ *Do you have a business plan and financial projections for the actual territory?*
▶ *When do you plan to get started?*

Insight

If you are determined to start a business you cannot afford, sweat equity may be the answer. You need to find a business partner who puts up the initial funding. You work in the business, draw a relatively small salary but are entitled to a share of the profits which you use to buy the investor out over time.

RAISING FINANCE – PROSPECTIVE FRANCHISOR

If a prospective franchisor requires funding to prepare the business for expansion through franchising, the banker is likely to assess the loan proposal like any other request for expansion finance. At this stage, franchising hasn't brought its magic to bear and you will have to convince the banker that the project has merit. Preparing answers to the questions listed in the following table will help you do that.

Questions a banker may ask prospective franchisors

- ▶ *Company's registered name and trademark details.*
- ▶ *Company's address and contact details.*
- ▶ *Personal name, address and contact details.*
- ▶ *Company structure.*

- ▶ *What is your company's main field of activity and trading history?*
- ▶ *Is the product that forms the basis for the franchise new, or does it have an established market?*
- ▶ *Do you currently sell the product locally, regionally or nationally?*
- ▶ *If you answered 'locally', how do you know that demand exists throughout the country?*
- ▶ *If your operation depends on the supply of inputs that are in short supply, will your current suppliers be able to cope with the increase in demand you will create or are there alternatives?*
- ▶ *Is the main product seasonal – if so, how will franchisees survive during off-seasons?*
- ▶ *What is the overall status of the industry-sector – now – over the next five to seven years?*
- ▶ *Who are your company's main competitors and what are their main strengths/weaknesses?*
- ▶ *Who are the company's main suppliers?*
- ▶ *Is vertical integration an issue in this sector, or could it become one in the foreseeable future?*

▶ *Do you have any practical experience in franchising?*
▶ *Are you fully aware of your rights and responsibilities as a franchisor?*
▶ *What makes you think that your business can be franchised?*
▶ *Why do you believe that franchising may be the best available option?*
▶ *Did you undertake a feasibility study into the viability of the franchise operation, based on a franchise development plan?*
▶ *Did you undertake a feasibility study into the viability of franchised outlets based on experience garnered in your company-owned unit and/or pilot unit?*
▶ *Have you discussed this project with professional advisers?*
▶ *Did you receive franchise enquiries in the past?*
▶ *Are you prepared to develop the concept in accordance with tried and tested guidelines?*
▶ *Are you confident that it will be easy to attract suitable candidates as franchisees and train them in all facets of the business?*
▶ *Will you be seeking membership of the local franchise association?*

▶ *What is the total projected investment in the franchise project?*
▶ *How do you propose to fund this?*
▶ *Will you require the full loan upfront or do you wish to draw on it in stages?*
▶ *By when do you expect to break even/achieve profitability and how would you deal with possible delays in reaching this point?*
▶ *How do you propose to repay the loan?*

A final word on financial aspects

A franchise, if developed and implemented correctly, can become highly profitable over time. I need to reiterate, however, that a franchise is not, and never will be, a quick road to easy riches. People who enter the franchise arena under this assumption will be disappointed. To make money in franchising requires dedication, hard work and, above all, plenty of patience.

▶ *From the franchisor's perspective, franchising offers entrepreneurs with passion an opportunity to develop a small business into a national network much faster than would otherwise be possible.*
▶ *Franchising's synergies offer prospective franchisees a chance to own a small business of their own while being able to operate under a well-known trademark and enjoy access to a range of benefits that are normally accessible only to branches of large corporations.*

Enlightened bankers have recognized the advantages franchising offers and are generally more than willing to fund promising franchise concepts, often at preferential rates. Even during an economic downturn, bankers know that the strong support infrastructure franchised networks enjoy make them a safer proposition. This enables shrewd entrepreneurs to leverage their start-up capital. As mentioned earlier, the UK government is supportive of the concept. It provides, currently through the BIS Small Firms Loan Guarantee scheme, guarantees that reduce the need for collateral. Similar schemes are available in many other countries.

THE TEN MOST IMPORTANT THINGS YOU NEED TO REMEMBER

1 *Prospective franchisees need to familiarize themselves properly with the financial obligations they are about to incur before they sign a franchise agreement.*

2 *Seen from the prospective franchisee's viewpoint, upfront fee levels and ongoing fee percentages are of less importance than the value of the brand and the amount of support the franchisor offers.*

3 *If the success of the franchise is highly location-dependant and suitable sites are not readily available, any deposit the prospective franchisee is asked to pay should be paid into a properly constituted trust account.*

4 *An obligation to purchase goods from the franchisor or a supplier prescribed by the franchisor should offer the franchisee genuine savings. The price must be right and the franchisee must not be forced to purchase goods in excess of actual requirements.*

5 *Excessive borrowing is the most frequent cause for business failure. This is the reason why no responsible franchisor will accept an individual as a franchisee unless he or she can make a reasonable contribution to the total funding requirements.*

6 *Commercial banks love franchising because they know that a franchisee of a reputable brand constitutes a better credit risk than an independent operator.*

7 *To enhance his or her chances of success in obtaining bank finance, a prospective franchisee must prepare a well thought out business plan and ask for the correct type of finance and the right amount.*

8 *Banks don't grant loans because they feel sorry for an applicant. It follows that the banker does not want to see the applicant grovel but wants to be convinced that the business idea has merit and that the applicant has the ability to make a success of the business.*

9 *A prospective franchisor needs to prove the viability of the business at its own expense before offering franchises to others. It is widely accepted that to offer an untested idea as a franchise and collect franchise fees borders on fraud.*

10 *A prospective franchisor needs to accept that to launch the programme will require a substantial injection of capital. Following the launch, the franchise is likely to operate at a loss. It usually takes three to five years before a franchise operation generates profits.*

4

The franchise agreement and related issues

In this chapter you will learn:
- *how the law deals with franchise arrangements*
- *the rights and obligations the franchise agreement should set out*
- *what role the operations and procedures manual plays*
- *what the franchisor should disclose to qualified prospects*
- *how disputes between a franchisor and a franchisee should be resolved*

This chapter deals with the legal implications of franchising and explains the main points a franchise agreement needs to cover. Other issues to be explored include the franchisor's obligation to provide full disclosure, the link between the franchise agreement and the network's operations manual and some methods of dispute resolution.

What does the law say?

Although franchising as a method of doing business is now well entrenched in most countries around the world, only a few have seen the need to put specific franchise legislation in place. The rationale for this has always been that because franchising is a commercial arrangement, franchise agreements should be drafted according to the rules of existing commercial law.

Feedback received from the USA where franchise legislation was introduced early on suggests that in an ideal world, this would be the correct approach and should be maintained. Once a country's legislature begins to regulate a complex commercial process like franchising, entrepreneurship development stands to suffer and compliance costs tend to go through the roof.

It was mainly for these reasons that governments in most countries were content to accept self-regulation of the sector by a representative body of peers. They thought that if people who are familiar with the franchise sector's needs and have a vested interested in keeping it 'clean' develop appropriate guidelines, the odds of achieving positive outcomes would be better than if a legislative jackboot approach were applied. Self-regulation worked well enough for a time, but unfortunately the actions of a few less than honourable players who entered the sector seeking quick and easy riches caused an increasing number of gullible individuals to suffer significant financial losses.

As a result, although the vast majority of franchisors conducted their businesses according to the rules of the game, pressure on governments to regulate the sector increased and a growing number have done so. Within the EU, for example, France, Spain and Italy have enacted franchise legislation already and there is no telling which country will be next.

Up to now, the UK has stayed true to the path of self-regulation, as have many other countries. The national franchise association's Code of Ethics for Franchising serve as the de-facto guide for ethical franchising. The downside of this approach is that franchise associations lack the power to regulate the conduct of non-members. They can only:

▶ *Withhold accreditation from franchisors who are found wanting;*
▶ *Withdraw accreditation from members who misbehave by, for example, failing to adhere to the Code of Ethics for Franchising.*

The BFA's claim that it is safer to deal with franchisors who are members of this organization has merit. This does not mean that the franchise offer of a franchisor who is not a member of the BFA is automatically suspect. However, if you are a prospective franchisee and you come across such a franchisor you should take extra care to ensure that the network's approach conforms with the basic criteria for ethical franchising. You will read more about this topic in the next chapter where I provide guidelines for the evaluation of franchise offers.

For access to the full text of the BFA's Code of Ethics for Franchising, visit the website www.thebfa.org.uk.

Tip

A franchise is granted, never sold. What you are paying for is the right to use the franchisor's intellectual property in accordance with the franchisor's operational guidelines. The moment the franchise arrangement comes to an end, this right evaporates.

The franchise agreement

Although the relationship between the franchisor and its franchisees is an intensely personal one, its complexity is such that it needs to be placed on a sound legal footing. This is done through the franchise agreement, potentially the most important agreement you will ever sign. I must caution that it is not the aim of this section to turn you into an expert on franchise agreements. This would neither be feasible nor advisable.

Working through this section will help you to understand the most important issues involved in signing a franchise agreement but before you sign one, or indeed any other agreement that is linked to a proposed franchise venture, you need to consult with a solicitor. Not just any solicitor, mind you, but a solicitor with proven expertise in franchise matters. Contact the local franchise association in your country for a referral; you'll find contact details in Chapter 7.

I have come across instances where prospective franchisees saved money by signing a franchise agreement without seeking professional advice. When things didn't work out, they asked me to help. In most instances, it was too late. As the Americans say: 'A man who acts as his own attorney has a fool for a client.'

FRANCHISE AGREEMENTS ARE NON-NEGOTIABLE

Although some solicitors may tell you otherwise, widespread agreement exists that the franchise agreement should not be negotiable. This is how it should be, assuming of course that it has been drafted properly in the first place. Should it be inherently flawed, the franchisor needs to have it redrafted. At that point, it should be offered to every prospective and existing franchisee in the network.

Should the franchisor's refusal to negotiate the clauses of the franchise agreement seem unreasonable to you, consider this: For a franchised network to function properly, it needs to operate according to one set of rules. Presumably, these rules were laid down after careful consideration of their merits. The franchise agreement should reflect these rules and balance them with the legitimate concerns of franchisor and franchisee. Once this has been achieved, the agreement should become the de facto standard until fundamental changes, be they internal or external, dictate otherwise.

Important note
From the franchisor's viewpoint, to accede to a prospective franchisee's request to change the franchise agreement would set a dangerous precedent. It would not make sense either.

► *Uniformity, a pillar of brand building and a hallmark of franchising, would be lost because, for example, changes to the contract might permit one franchisee to vary aspects of product range and customer service.*
► *With every franchisee operating under a different agreement, franchisee management would become an absolute nightmare.*

► *Dissatisfaction among members of the network would be rife because everyone would suspect that the other was granted more favourable terms.*

SUBSTANTIAL AGREEMENT

Should you be unfamiliar with franchise agreements, you might be surprised to learn that it is a complex agreement, frequently running to 60 or more pages. This is necessary because the franchise agreement deals with a multitude of issues including the grant of the franchise, property rights and lease provisions, the respective rights and obligations of the franchisor and the franchisee and what will happen should the franchisee wish to sell the business or die. The consequences of one or the other party defaulting on the agreement or the agreement coming to an end for some other reason will also be set out.

BALANCED AGREEMENT

Before I delve into the clauses you are likely to find in a typical franchise agreement, I need to explain one important difference between a franchise agreement and any other commercial agreement. To maintain the spirit of franchising intact, a franchise agreement should be balanced and fair. It needs to reflect the interests of both parties in almost equal measure. I say 'almost' for a reason because, in the interest of the network as a whole, it needs to give the franchisor some overriding powers. The reason for this is that the franchisor acts in a dual capacity:

1 *The franchisor has developed the concept and is entitled to safeguard and protect its own commercial interests.*
2 *The franchisor has a moral obligation to protect the interests of other members of the network against the ill-conceived actions of franchisees who fail to adhere to the network's operating procedures.*

The following example shows why this is necessary.

Tyre King is a tyre fitment franchise with over 200 outlets. The network differentiates itself from its competitors by delivering outstanding service, and its ongoing marketing campaigns stress this point. However, one franchisee, let's call him John, is less than diligent in meeting the level of service standards Tyre King's customers have come to expect. Not surprisingly, John's business produces mediocre results but the impact of his failure to perform goes further than that. Seeing that John traded under the network's brand, he tarnished the entire network's reputation. Had the franchisor stood idly by, the brand would have lost value, to the detriment of the franchisor and other franchisees in the network. John refused to accept the franchisor's offers of assistance which he perceived as interference. After several fruitless attempts to put the matter right, the franchisor had no option but to terminate John's franchise agreement. A harsh step but a necessary one!

Remember: The franchisor, being the custodian of the brand, is morally obliged to protect it against the consequences of ill-considered actions by franchisees.

The spirit of the franchise agreement

I have already said that the franchise agreement must enable the franchisor to protect the brand and exercise control over the performance of all members of the network. This means that the franchisor must hold the balance of power. However, in the spirit of the win–win outcome that franchising promises, the franchisor's powers must be carefully balanced against the need to meet the long-term expectations of the network's growing number of franchisees. In other words, the franchise agreement should be drafted in such a way that it takes the interests of both parties into account.

This is a departure from the cutthroat world of commercial agreements in general, where one frequently comes across agreements that patently favour one party over the other. Solicitors with experience in franchise matters know that in franchising, agreements that fail to address franchisees' legitimate concerns will not work. They may even lead to the demise of a network.

As soon as a franchisee gets the feeling that he or she is trapped in an inequitable agreement, they are likely to seek support from fellow-franchisees and no confidentiality clause will stop him or her from doing just that. Before long, several franchisees who share the initiator's concerns will group together to challenge the fairness of the franchise agreement. Once this happens, discontent among franchisees is likely to spread throughout the network. This will eventually lead to an irreversible breakdown of trust. The resulting working climate will make it impossible for the franchisor to continue cooperation with its franchisees and the network will fall apart.

Insight

Little can be worse than having an unhappy franchisee in the network. To minimize the chance of this happening to them, I advise my franchisor clients to grant prospective franchisees a cooling-off period of 14 days. This period starts when the franchise agreement is signed and allows the new franchisee to change his or her mind without incurring any penalties. Some national franchise associations have made this practice binding on members.

THE PARTIES TO THE FRANCHISE AGREEMENT

In a strictly legal sense, every franchise agreement is entered into between a franchisor and one specific franchisee. What is frequently overlooked, however, is the fact that three other parties will be affected to a greater or lesser extent. Unless the franchise agreement enables the franchisor to exercise adequate control over the way each franchisee operates, the entire network, its suppliers and customers could suffer. This could be the result of the ill-considered actions of just one errant franchisee.

▶ *The franchisor, having invested much time and money in the creation of the franchise package, is entitled to protect the value of the network's brand and ensure its continued growth.*

▶ *Other franchisees within the network will rely on the reputation of the brand to help them in their efforts to maximize market penetration and with it, their business results.*

▶ *The network's suppliers, who may have entered into network-wide supply agreements at preferential terms, will expect each member of the network to meet its obligations. Should, for example, one franchisee habitually default on payments, the credit rating of all other members of the network could be negatively affected.*

▶ *In response to the brand's advertising message, guided by their own past experiences and influenced by 'word of mouth', customers tend to develop certain expectations when dealing with a brand. They may not know which store within a network is company-owned and which one is franchised, nor will they really care. They expect that the service experience offered under the banner of the brand remains consistent throughout, no matter where the outlet they choose to frequent is located or who the owner is. If this simple expectation is not met, the brand stands to suffer.*

Important note

The franchise agreement must give the franchisor the power to enforce adherence to the steps required to ensure that all members of the network meet the expectations of the network's stakeholders.

WHAT DOES THE FRANCHISE AGREEMENT COVER?

A typical franchise agreement should, subject to the needs of a particular industry sector, contain provisions that deal with some or all of the following issues.

Identity of the parties
▶ *To begin with, this clause will give details of the franchisor.*
▶ *It will also state whether the franchisee is an individual, a partnership or a company, and provide all relevant information, for example the company registration number in the case of a registered business, or personal details if the franchisee is a private individual.*

Definition of ownership
This clause should explain in no uncertain terms who owns what in the arrangement.

▶ *The franchisee is usually the owner of the franchised business. This includes furniture and fittings, equipment, stock and any other assets required to operate the business on a day-to-day basis.*
▶ *The franchisor retains ownership of the network's corporate identity including its trademark and the network's other intellectual property. Examples of the latter are the network's tried and tested systems and proprietary methods of performing certain tasks.*
▶ *To qualify for protection, confidential methods the franchisor has developed and allows the franchisee to use need to be recorded. This is usually done in the network's operations manual.*

Grant of the franchise
A franchise is granted, never sold. Typically, franchisees will be licensed to operate one or a specified number of units of the franchise, either at a specific address or within a clearly defined

territory. The licence will entitle the franchisee to use the system's brand name(s) and corporate image, sometimes known as the get-up, as well as its know-how as described in the franchise agreement and the operations manual.

This licence is usually issued for a fixed period and is not absolute. Should the franchisee fail to adhere to the terms of the grant, the franchisor will have the right to withdraw it. Although the grant constitutes only one of the many facets of the franchise arrangement, it nevertheless deals with several complex issues.

TERM OF THE FRANCHISE
This clause reflects the following arrangements:

- *The duration of the initial term.*
- *The initial term is usually five to ten years but can be as long as 20 years. It will depend on the amount of investment and store lease arrangements. As a minimum requirement, the duration of the agreement, the period it takes the franchisee to repay loans and the duration of the store lease must match.*
- *Some networks offer open-ended agreements that are fixed for a specified period then continue indefinitely. Once this stage has been reached, each party is entitled to give the other notice, subject to agreed conditions.*
- *Renewal right in favour of the franchisee: It is customary to grant the franchisee an option to renew the agreement on its expiry, usually for an identical period. Renewal may be conditional upon the franchisee meeting certain requirements. It could, for example, depend on the franchisee having achieved certain performance criteria; if so, these should be listed.*
- *Another requirement that is often included is that the franchisee upgrades the unit's corporate image to bring it in line with the network's standards at the time of renewal.*
- *Some franchisors insist that franchisees sign a new agreement, identical to the one offered to new franchisees at the time the*

*renewal takes place. This needs to be stated while making it
clear that further renewals will not automatically be granted.*

▶ *Should a renewal fee become payable then this must be disclosed
in the initial agreement. Given the long term of the initial
agreement and taking the possibility of inflation into account, it
may be difficult to state an absolute figure. This can be overcome
by stating, for example, that the renewal fee is 50 per cent of the
initial fee payable at the time the agreement comes up for renewal.*

TERRITORIAL RIGHTS

The franchise agreement will define the territory for which the
franchise is being granted.

▶ *This may be limited to a specific address or a clearly defined
area surrounding a specific location. This can be expressed
in the form of a distance, for example, a five-mile radius
measured from the centre of a specified landmark building, a
specified number of postcode areas or a specified county.*

▶ *Prudent franchisors will balance franchisees' desire to be
granted access to a large territory with the need to ensure a
high degree of market penetration.*

▶ *One option is to grant a franchisee a certain territory and
link this grant to an option to acquire one or more adjoining
territories within a specified period. This option is likely to be
conditional upon the franchisee reaching specified sales levels
or other performance criteria in the original area.*

▶ *If territorial exclusivity is granted then this must be set out.
It should be mentioned that such a grant could be vulnerable
to attack under competition law, potentially rendering the
franchisor powerless to enforce it.*

USE OF THE CORPORATE IMAGE

The grant will provide for the fitting out of the premises and how
the brand is to be represented. Detailed guidelines will usually
be contained in the operations manual or in a dedicated set-up
manual. These things need to be mentioned here.

Initial obligations of the franchisee

FINANCIAL OBLIGATIONS

▶ *To pay the prescribed initial fee and to fund the establishment of the unit as well as a store opening campaign. This clause will also contain a payment schedule.*

▶ *The terms linked to the payment of an initial deposit, and conditions applying to possible full or partial refunds, as the case may be, need to be explained.*

GENERAL OBLIGATIONS

▶ *To attend training at a location specified by the franchisor; should it be necessary that the franchisee's key staff participate in this training, this needs to be stated.*

▶ *In suitable circumstances, to enter into a lease agreement for a site approved by the franchisor.*

▶ *To make the business ready for trading. This will usually be done in close cooperation with the franchisor. If so, it needs to be stated.*

▶ *To employ and train staff.*

▶ *To comply with all legal and statutory requirements of operating the business as set out in the operations manual.*

▶ *To maintain utmost good faith and confidentiality in all dealings with the franchisor.*

Initial obligations of the franchisor

▶ *To provide the franchisee with a tried and tested product range, business system and corporate identity package.*

▶ *To train the franchisee in all aspects of operating the business and assist him or her with setting up procedures and related issues, for example:*

▷ *The raising of funds. Many franchisors have arrangements with one or more of the high street banks which could be made accessible to franchisees. However, franchisees should not be obliged to utilize the franchisor's funding arrangements.*

▷ *Site selection, lease negotiations, specifications for the fitting-out of the unit and compliance with statutory obligations.*

▷ *The purchase and commissioning of equipment,
   introduction to key suppliers and the provision of
   specifications for the purchase of opening stock in
   appropriate mix and quantities.*
▷ *Staff selection and training.*
▷ *Planning and implementation of a 'grand opening'.*
▷ *Initial trouble-shooting assistance.*
▷ *Detailed operating guidelines, set out in writing in one
   or more operations manuals (see the paragraph headed
   'The relationship between the franchise agreement and the
   operations manual' later in this chapter).*

COMPULSORY PURCHASING ARRANGEMENTS
Should the franchisee be under an obligation to purchase goods
either from the franchisor or from suppliers designated by the
franchisor, this must be set out in the agreement.

▶ *Contractual requirements to purchase minimum amounts of
   merchandise should set alarm bells ringing in the minds of the
   franchisee and his or her advisers.*
▶ *In the interest of fairness, this clause should provide
   safeguards protecting the franchisee against exploitation.*

Franchisee's ongoing obligations
The franchise agreement is likely to deal with the franchisee's
ongoing commitments in broad brushstrokes only. Details will
be set out in the operations manual. By way of example, the
franchisee may be obliged to:

▶ *Adhere to prescribed processes and procedures as detailed in
   the operations manual.*
▶ *Offer the range of products and services prescribed by the
   franchisor and maintain adequate stock levels and/or service
   capacity at all times.*
▶ *Manage the business hands-on during prescribed minimum
   opening hours.*

► *Staff the business with competent individuals and maintain prescribed minimum staffing levels throughout official opening hours. Related requirements may be to:*
  ▷ *Select staff in accordance with the franchisor's recruitment guidelines.*
  ▷ *Provide adequate training and supervision of staff.*
  ▷ *Forge a productive team by creating a positive working climate and offering deserving members of staff opportunities for advancement.*
► *Participate in national advertising campaigns.*
  ▷ *Support national campaigns by stocking the appropriate merchandise and linking the theme of local promotions to that of national activities.*
  ▷ *Spend a set minimum amount on local advertising, keeping in mind that prior to placement, local advertising must always be approved by head office.*
► *Conduct all business affairs in a proper fashion.*
  ▷ *Keep proper books of account, comply with statutory requirements and submit certain reports by specific dates.*
  ▷ *Pay all amounts due to the franchisor by due date. Examples are weekly or monthly management services fees, contribution to the advertising or marketing fund, payments resulting from product supplies, etc. The basis for the calculation of such amounts and the setting of due dates must be given.*
  ▷ *Pay all amounts due to creditors by due date.*
► *Participate fully in all programmes arranged by the franchisor for the benefit of franchisees and/or the network as a whole. Details can be given in the operations manual but should costs be involved, the basis on which these costs will be calculated should be stated in the agreement. Examples are:*
  ▷ *Cooperating with the network's field service representatives and other franchisor personnel.*
  ▷ *Participation in training sessions arranged for the franchisee and/or the franchisee's staff.*
  ▷ *Participation in regional or national meetings, workshops or seminars.*

- *Represent the brand with enthusiasm and pride, for example:*
  - ▷ *The franchisee will refrain from taking any action that could damage the standing of the brand, especially but not only in the eyes of the target market.*
  - ▷ *Notify the franchisor at once should the brand come under attack.*
- *Should a Franchisee Representative Committee or similar body exist, the franchisee will be required to participate in its activities.*

Franchisor's ongoing obligations

- *The franchiswwor is obliged to provide ongoing support to franchisees in good standing, for example:*
  - ▷ *A support facility that is immediately available to franchisees should an emergency arise. At the very least, availability should be guaranteed throughout the network's normal business hours. Depending on the nature of the business, this might involve telephonic support, ad hoc visits by technical experts and/or appropriate arrangements with third-party suppliers.*
  - ▷ *Planned visits; these should include:*
    - ▷ *Regular corporate identity and product quality audits.*
    - ▷ *Business performance reviews and mentoring sessions.*
  - ▷ *It should be reflected that store visits will be conducted in a spirit of cooperation and improvement. Practicalities permitting, the proposed minimum frequency of such visits should be laid down in the agreement.*
  - ▷ *The arranging of training sessions for the benefit of franchisees and their staff. Practicalities permitting, the proposed minimum frequency of such training sessions should be laid down in the agreement.*
  - ▷ *Negotiation of bulk deals for the benefit of franchisees.*
  - ▷ *Aggressive marketing and brand building efforts.*

General provisions

- *Conditions for the implementation of systems modifications.*
  - ▷ *An obligation to implement systems improvements developed by the franchisor.*

- ▷ Conditions for the approval of systems improvements developed and proposed by the franchisee.
- ▷ Intellectual property rights issues arising from the involvement of franchisees in systems improvements.
- ▶ Nature and extent of the restraint of trade the franchisee may be bound by, for example:
  - ▷ Some franchisors will insist that throughout the period the franchise agreement is in force, the franchisee channels all his or her time and attention into the operation of the franchise.
  - ▷ Other franchisors permit their franchisees' involvement in other business activities as long as they don't create a conflict of interest by competing with the franchise.
  - ▷ After expiry of the franchise agreement, the franchisee will be prohibited from operating a business in opposition to the network. This portion of the restraint will normally be limited, both in regard to the territory it covers and its duration.
  - ▷ Conditions governing the transfer of control over the franchise. This would cover:
    - ▷ The transfer of control over the franchised unit to a manager. Should the franchisor agree to this, it is customary to make this conditional upon the franchisor approving the individual's appointment. The incoming manager may also be compelled to undergo appropriate training and to sign a confidentiality undertaking in favour of the franchisor.
    - ▷ The proposed sale of the unit by the franchisee. It is customary for the franchisor to insist that the buyer meets the network's selection criteria for new franchisees.
    - ▷ Some franchisors insist on the insertion of a clause giving them the right of first refusal. This means that should the franchisee wish to sell, the franchisor has to be given a period to decide whether it wants to acquire the unit. Should you come across this clause, you need to ensure that the method of fixing the price is fair.
    - ▷ Provisions dealing with the eventuality of the franchisee's death.

- ▶ *Clauses dealing with the enforcement of the contract, for example:*
  - ▷ *Definition of 'breach of contract'; this clause will define: What constitutes a breach?*
  - ▷ *Which breaches can be remedied? This clause will include an outline of the process to be followed, for example the method of notification of the breach and time to be allowed for rectification, consequences of failure to remedy and what would happen in cases of frequent repetition.*
  - ▷ *Which breaches cannot be remedied? A franchisor might, for example, see an instance of fee fraud committed by a franchisee as a breach that cannot be remedied because trust has been lost.*
- ▶ *Provision for the mediation or arbitration of disputes:*
  - ▷ *The process to be followed in the appointment of the mediator or arbitrator.*
  - ▷ *Selection of the individual and the venue.*
  - ▷ *Allocation of costs arising from the dispute resolution process.*
  - ▷ *What will happen should the process be unsuccessful?*
- ▶ *Termination of the agreement.*
  - ▷ *Termination could be the result of:*
    - ▷ *The agreement coming to a natural end because the contract period has expired.*
    - ▷ *The agreement having been terminated by one party in response to a breach of contract by the other.*
  - ▷ *Consequences of termination: For the affected party, the consequences of termination can be severe. For this reason, they need to be set out clearly and without ambiguity. Should the franchisor terminate the franchise agreement, its minimum demands are likely to include the following:*
    - ▷ *Cessation of trading under the network's name.*
    - ▷ *Immediate removal of all items of corporate identity.*
    - ▷ *Return to the franchisor of all manuals, customer lists and other confidential materials.*

▷ *Some franchisors will insist on the franchisee vacating the premises and/or selling the equipment used in the business to the franchisor. Given the circumstances, this would serve both parties' interests best subject to a fair settlement being offered.*

▷ *With the probability of an enforceable trade restraint looming large, the franchisee could not use the equipment; selling it to the franchisor would free him or her of this burden.*

▷ *The franchisor can easily use the equipment. Purchasing it from the former franchisee reduces the likelihood of contraventions against restraint clauses occurring.*

▷ *Should the franchisee hold proprietary stock (that is stock that is branded to reflect the network's corporate identity) realistic provisions need to be in place regarding its disposal at a fair price.*

Insight

Trade restraints should be enforced with sensitivity, keeping in mind that the ex-franchisee needs to be permitted to earn a living. This can be a balancing act because the network's interests need to be protected as well, especially if a new franchisee is to be appointed in the area.

Standard contract clauses

In addition to a host of clauses that are specific to the franchise relationship, franchise agreements will contain a number of standard contract clauses, for example:

▶ *An explanation of the relationship between the parties. This clause will usually state that the parties are independent entities and neither is entitled to bind the other in any way.*

▶ *A statement that neither party will rely upon representations made by the other unless these are reflected in the agreement, or in a side letter.*

▶ *An affirmation by the franchisee that he or she understands that the franchisor does not warrant the franchisee's success but that this will depend on the hard work, ability and dedication of the franchisee.*

▶ *An acknowledgement by the franchisee that he or she has read the agreement in its entirety and understands its meaning.*

▶ *A confirmation by the franchisee that he or she has been encouraged by the franchisor to seek independent professional legal and accounting advice before signing this agreement.*

▶ *A statement to the effect that, should any clause contained in the agreement infringe against legislation that might exist already or come into force and effect at a later stage, the parties agree that this affects the offending clause only. The balance of the agreement would remain intact.*

▶ *Notifications and selection of competent court:*
  ▷ *The parties' respective delivery addresses for official notices will be stated, as well as the period after which the intended recipient of the notice is deemed to have received it.*
  ▷ *The agreement will state which party has the right to select a competent court.*

Insight

In my experience, the relationship between the franchisor and the franchisee cannot be conducted by waving the franchise agreement about. Once signed, the agreement should be securely filed away and allowed to collect dust. Should the one or other party feel the need to refer to the franchise agreement, chances are that something has gone seriously wrong.

The relationship between the franchise agreement and the operations manual

It is in the nature of a franchise arrangement that the franchise agreement is a bulky document. Just imagine how much more complex it would become if the franchisor used it to cover every conceivable operational detail. To keep the franchise agreement manageable and avoid the unacceptable burden of having to renegotiate the agreement every time a change in day-to-day operational requirements becomes necessary, only the broad principles according to which the network operates are recorded in the agreement.

This is linked to a proviso which clearly states that the detailed operational requirements are set out in a series of written directives. These will be issued by the franchisor and delivered to the franchisee in the form of one or more operations manuals. Once the manual has been issued, the franchisor is obliged to issue updates so that changes in operational requirements are reflected. As soon as such updates are received by the franchisee, they become binding just as if they were contained in an amendment to the franchise agreement.

However, this provision cannot be used by the franchisor to unilaterally make material changes to the franchise agreement. The two examples that follow will illustrate this.

Example 1: Staff uniforms
A clause contained in the franchise agreement obliges franchisees to compel their staff to wear corporate uniforms prescribed by the franchisor. To maintain the appeal of the corporate identity, the franchisor may from time to time issue updates to the operations manual that change the style and colour of these uniforms. On receipt of such updates, the franchisee will be contractually bound to implement the new image.

Example 2: Management services fee
According to your franchise agreement, the management services fee you are obliged to pay is calculated as 5 per cent of net sales and you have entered into the franchise agreement on this basis. Any change to this fee level might affect the commercial viability of your franchise and would therefore be classified as a material contract change.

Should your franchisor realize at a later date that it has underestimated the costs of providing ongoing franchisee support and wants to increase the fee level, it cannot do this by simply publishing an update to the operations manual. Such a change would require the drafting of a formal addendum to the original franchise agreement that would have to be agreed to and signed by the franchisee before it would become binding.

Tip

Franchise agreements are complex documents; never ever sign one without obtaining expert advice first. To pay the £500 or whatever it costs to have the agreement properly explained to you by an expert is preferable to signing it without fully understanding its implications. The law does not recognize ignorance as a valid defence!

Issues surrounding disclosure

One of the greatest problems facing prospective franchisees is to ensure they are fully aware of what they let themselves in for when they invest in a franchise. Although this is the exception rather than the rule, incidents are on record where people have lost their investment, or have found themselves locked into an unworkable contract with untrustworthy people, either because of misrepresentation on the part of a self-styled franchisor, or because they failed to investigate the opportunity properly.

The prospective franchisor is not the only entity you need to investigate. It does not really matter how well a network is managed, if you get accepted into it only to find that it is not what you expected, the resulting damage can be great. Quite clearly, careful investigation is necessary before you sign a franchise agreement. I will deal with this at length in Chapter 5.

For the moment, we'll focus on the documentation franchisors can be expected to make available to qualified franchisee prospects.

In the United States, every franchisor is under a legal obligation to produce a Uniform Franchise Offering Circular, known as an UFOC. This is a substantial document that tells prospective franchisees everything they need to know about the business, ranging from the network's history to its financial standing. It will also contain a copy of the franchise agreement. Once a prospective franchisee has worked through the UFOC, he or she will be able to base their decision about joining the network on hard facts.

Franchisors are obliged to update the UFOC regularly and file a copy with a government body. They wouldn't dare to be less than forthright in their disclosure because this could have serious legal repercussions for them.

In several other countries, government agencies and/or the national franchise associations compel franchisors to produce formal disclosure documents. Broadly speaking, requirements for their compilation are less stringent than those pertaining to the UFOC but they provide prospective franchisees with peace of mind. Following this paragraph an example of guidelines for the creation of such a document, in this case issued by the Franchise Association of South Africa. Although this document has absolutely no bearing on the situation in any other country, it outlines the type of information you might want to request from a prospective franchisor.

Requirements for the creation of a disclosure document

1 *Full and traceable information about the franchisor company including contact details and details of professional affiliations.*

2   Details of qualifications and business experience of the
    franchisor and its officers, firstly, in the type of business being
    offered as a franchise and secondly, in the operation of a
    franchise.
3   Details of criminal or civil action against the franchisor or
    its officers, either taken during the past three years or still
    pending.
4   Full details of the franchise offer and the actual product or
    service it is based on.
5   Full details of the obligations of the franchisor vis-a-vis the
    franchisee.
6   Full details of the obligations of the franchisee vis-à-vis the
    franchisor.
7   An explanation of the most important clauses of the franchise
    agreement, including restrictions placed on the franchisee.
8   Financial projections for at least two years and an explanation
    of the basis on which these projections were calculated.
9   Full details of all payments, initial and ongoing, the franchisee
    will be expected to make, and what he can expect to receive in
    return for these payments.
10 A list of existing franchisees and their contact details.
11 An auditor's certificate confirming that the franchisor's
    business is a going concern and likely to be able to meet its
    obligations as they fall due. This needs to be supplemented by
    a statement made by a senior franchisor representative to the
    effect that to his or her best knowledge and belief, the financial
    situation of the franchise company has not deteriorated since
    the day the auditor's certificate was issued.
12 The disclosure document needs to be updated at least annually,
    more frequently, should material changes occur.

*** These are the minimum requirements for the compilation
of a disclosure document imposed by a national franchise
association on its members.** Please note that this document
has absolutely no standing in the UK and is reproduced for
information purposes only.

BREACH OF CONFIDENTIALITY

Initially, ethical franchisors in those countries where the issue of a disclosure document has, for all practical purposes, become mandatory, supported this requirement wholeheartedly. They soon found out to their dismay that compliance made them vulnerable to commercial espionage. Acting in good faith, they had handed copies of disclosure documents and franchise agreements to individuals who had presented themselves as prospective franchisees. Unfortunately, some of the recipients had ulterior motives.

The disclosure document contains confidential information about the network's business activities and financial performance. By pretending to be interested in a franchisor's opportunity, some less than honourable individuals obtained the documentation so that they could pass it on to the franchisor's competitors. Alternatively, they attempted to use it for their own purposes.

To protect themselves against such blatant breach of trust, most franchisors now expect prospects to sign a confidentiality undertaking before handing over a disclosure document. The only obligation a properly worded confidentiality agreement should impose upon a prospect is to observe confidentiality and not to use the information for any other purpose but to assess the opportunity.

THE SITUATION IN THE UK

Although there is currently no obligation on UK franchisors to produce a formal disclosure document, some franchisors do so voluntary. Members of the BFA are in any event compelled to furnish prospective franchisees with comprehensive information on the viability of the opportunity and submit this documentation to the BFA for scrutiny.

There is also a legal threat. Should a franchisee find out the hard way that the franchisor has misrepresented the financial situation of the franchise, or the earnings potential of the opportunity, he or she would be entitled to turn to the courts for relief. This would apply even if the franchisor had inserted a disclaimer into their financial projections and their franchise agreements.

Let me give you an example: A franchisor's financial projections create the impression that a new franchisee can expect to achieve £2 000 000 in sales during his or her first year of operation. It later turns out that actual sales achieved in the past by new units operating in areas with similar demographics have never exceeded the £500 000 mark. This could be seen as deliberate misrepresentation. Should a franchisee be able to convince a court that he or she has entered into the franchise agreement on the strength of such misrepresentation, the agreement could be set aside, plus damages may be awarded to the franchisee.

Important note

In the example given above, I suggest that a franchisee who was the victim of deliberate misrepresentation should seek relief from a court. Seeing that in the next paragraph I recommend alternative methods of dispute resolution, you might find this advice ironic. It's a matter of 'horses for courses'. Most ordinary disputes between franchisor and franchisee are best resolved through negotiation. Deliberate misrepresentation is a different matter altogether and hardly likely to be resolved by talking about it.

Alternative methods of dispute resolution

The relationship between franchisor and franchisee should be mutually supportive, and indeed it is – at least most of the time. If you consider the vast numbers of franchisors and franchisees that are in operation by now, it should not surprise you to learn that on occasion, disputes do arise. It can happen in the best-managed systems and should never be seen as the end of the road.

The important thing is that disputes are dealt with in a fair and decisive manner. This is the only way they can be resolved without lasting damage to the relationship. To quote from the Code of Ethics for Franchising of the BFA, 'parties should resolve complaints, grievances and disputes with good faith and goodwill through fair and reasonable direct communication and negotiation'. But what happens if the direct approach doesn't work?

Several methods of dispute resolution are available, with the most popular option being mediation, followed by arbitration. In most instances, using either one of these methods is preferable to turning to the courts, especially if an ongoing working relationship between the franchisor and the franchisee needs to be preserved.

MEDIATION

Mediation is done under the guidance of an experienced mediator. Participation in the process is voluntary, in other words, neither the franchisor nor the franchisee can force the other to involve a mediator in their dispute. Agreement is usually achieved through a clause in the franchise agreement.

The mediator does not represent either party or defend its point of view; rather, he or she will endeavour to guide both parties towards reaching an acceptable solution. The mediator is in no position to impose a solution. It follows that, should the mediation attempt be unsuccessful, the matter will remain unresolved.

If the mediator is a professional practitioner, for example in the fields of law or accounting, he or she will probably charge a fee for the time spent on the mediation process. If so, responsibility for payment needs to be negotiated beforehand between the parties. In some countries, the national franchise association provides a mediation service. Turn to Chapter 7 for contact details.

ARBITRATION

This is a more formal process, and the findings of the arbitrator are usually binding. It follows that the arbitrator should be selected on the strength of his or her perceived ability to listen to both sides and come to a fair decision. For obvious reasons, retired judges are most often appointed as arbitrators, and the costs involved in arbitration can be substantial. It is important, therefore, to clarify upfront who will be responsible for what.

LEGAL PROCESS

In franchising, instances when parties become sufficiently aggrieved to turn to the courts for relief are fortunately rare. This is just as well because in most instances, legal proceedings are time-consuming and can become prohibitively expensive. You should also remember that with the best will in the world, your solicitor may not always be able to predict the outcome of a case with certainty. My advice: avoid taking matters to court if you possibly can.

Practical tips for the conduct of mediation proceedings

APPOINTING A MEDIATOR

The person appointed to mediate should be an individual both parties trust. Most often, a respected personality within the industry sector whose impartiality is beyond reproach is the most likely candidate.

CHOOSING A LOCATION

▶ *The venue should preferably be neutral. If its location forces one party to travel, the other party should have to travel as well.*
▶ *The availability of two separate rooms will facilitate progress.*

PROCESS

▶ *The mediator explains the ground rules, namely:*
  ▷ *to resolve the issue;*
  ▷ *to reaffirm common goals;*
  ▷ *to save the relationship.*
▶ *The mediator talks to party A in room 1; hears them out and records salient facts.*
▶ *The mediator talks to party B in room 2; hears them out and records salient facts.*
▶ *The mediator takes some time out to assess the facts and explore common ground. In complex cases, it may be necessary to adjourn.*
▶ *Once the mediator has gained a sound understanding of the underlying issues, he or she shuttles back and forth between rooms 1 and 2 to:*
  ▷ *obtain additional clarification;*
  ▷ *explain to each party where the other is coming from;*
  ▷ *explore the possibility of a compromise.*
▶ *As soon as the parties appear ready to settle the issue, the mediator brings them together in one room and facilitates a settlement.*
Please note that in the interest of brand integrity, no compromise will be possible when it comes to the upholding of operational standards.

THE TEN MOST IMPORTANT THINGS YOU NEED TO REMEMBER

1 *Only a few countries have specific franchise legislation in place but their number is growing all the time. In the absence of franchise legislation, a franchise arrangement is usually considered to be a normal commercial arrangement and treated as such by the courts.*

2 *National franchise associations publish a Code of Ethics and Business Practices which sets out how a bona fide franchise should operate. Such codes are usually binding on members of the franchise association only and have no legal standing. This notwithstanding, reference to a national code provides an insight into best franchising practices.*

3 *A good franchise agreement will be written in straightforward language everyone can understand; Latin terms, ambiguities and other solicitor-speak have no place in a franchise agreement.*

4 *In the interest of uniformity, the franchise agreement is generally not negotiable but should reflect the interests of both parties. Should the agreement contain a clause you cannot accept, don't ignore it or it will come back to haunt you. It is probably better to seek an opportunity elsewhere.*

5 *Although the franchise agreement needs to be balanced and fair, it needs to give the franchisor the power to protect the brand against ill-considered actions by errant franchisees. This is because the franchisor cannot be expect to stand idly by while a franchisee damages the brand.*

6 *The franchise agreement records the principles upon which the franchise relationship is built while detailed operational guidelines are contained in the operations manual. For these to become binding on franchisees, they must be underpinned by appropriate references in the franchise agreement.*

7 *In some countries, franchisors are obliged, either as a legal requirement or as a condition of membership to the national franchise association, to provide prospects with a disclosure document. In the absence of this requirement, progressive franchisors who have nothing to hide will comply voluntarily.*

8 *To avoid the devastating impact the presence of an unhappy franchisee can have on the network, forward-looking franchisors grant prospective franchisees a period to change their minds after they have signed the franchise agreement. This is known as a cooling-off period.*

9 *Franchisors who provide prospective franchisees with a disclosure document or make substantial disclosure in some other form have the right to insist on the prospect signing a formal confidentiality undertaking. Such an undertaking should not bind the prospect in any way beyond maintaining confidentiality.*

10 *Although disputes between a franchisor and one or more franchisees are fortunately rare, they do occur. In the spirit of franchising as well as to save costs, every reasonable effort should be made to resolve them outside the legal process. Arbitration or mediation are the most commonly used avenues.*

5

How to locate, evaluate and secure the right opportunity

In this chapter you will learn:
- *where to find franchise opportunities and do an initial evaluation*
- *what questions you should ask prospective franchisors*
- *why it is essential that you talk to existing franchisees*
- *what franchise models you may come across*

> 'If a man will begin with certainties, he shall end in doubt, but if he will be content to begin with doubts, he shall end in certainty.'
>
> Francis Bacon

Congratulations – you have made it through the boring stuff! You are now ready to begin your ascent towards business success by investigating franchise opportunities. In this chapter, I will show you how to locate opportunities that match your interests, skills and financial resources. Next, I will guide you through the process of creating a shortlist of promising opportunities and initiate contact. Other checklists will help you to find out everything you need to know by asking the right questions.

The best time to act is now!

Careful planning and evaluation are important steps but unless they are followed by decisive action, these activities will soon turn into aimless dreaming. I firmly believe that there has never been a better time to take the big step to business ownership than the here and now, and franchising is the best route to take. The following list, which is by no means exhaustive, tells you what makes me say that.

OPPORTUNITIES ARE AVAILABLE

▶ *Franchising has a reputation of being linked to fast food but this is an outdated notion. A quick visit to a website like www.whichfranchise.com will convince you that franchises are available in a multitude of sectors.*
▶ *Fierce competition forces an increasing number of companies to review their existing distribution networks. Their CEOs know that the implementation of customer satisfaction programmes stands and falls with the quality of the company's frontline people. They have come to recognize that franchisees are more likely to deliver service smartly and consistently than salaried managers. As a result, new franchise opportunities come on stream all the time.*
▶ *Established franchisors are eager to grow their networks and to accomplish that, they need a steady flow of quality franchisees.*

Instead of a shortage of opportunities being in evidence as was the case in the past, the tables have turned in favour of prospective franchisees. Competition for qualified prospects is heating up, and it's up to you to choose wisely.

Insight

Just like seasons change so does the economy. But while Mother Nature uses the winter months to rest, periods of economic downturn are no reason to sit back. In my view, they offer those who know how to spot bargains unlimited potential.

A FRANCHISE IS A DRAW CARD

► *Brand loyalty is on the increase. Customers prefer to deal with an outlet of a brand they know and trust rather than with an unknown entity.*
► *High street banks are willing to offer franchisees of recognized franchise networks preferential access to finance and banking services.*
► *Network-wide purchase arrangements put into place by franchisors for the benefit of their franchisees place small local units on an even footing with large national chains.*
► *It is easier to attract and retain good staff because people prefer to build their careers within the framework of a national brand.*

Lead generation

I have already said that far from being the sole domain of fast-food outlets, franchising has made inroads into a wide variety of industry sectors. You only need to walk through your town's high streets or shopping centres, and if you keep your eyes wide open, you will see franchise opportunities all around you. But while it may be comforting to know that you have such a large pool of opportunities to choose from, you need to be careful not to let this overwhelm you.

To avoid early burnout, focus on opportunities that genuinely interest you. Ignore those that have little appeal or are simply out of reach, for example because the investment threshold is too high. Be ruthless in your initial evaluation and you will soon end up with a manageable shortlist of genuine opportunities. Proceed as follows:

Ask for referrals
You can locate opportunities simply by walking around town, talking to people. Just let them know that you are in the market for a business opportunity under franchise. As most franchised networks

offer some form of territorial protection, an existing franchisee is unlikely to perceive you as a potential competitor. On the contrary, most franchisees are intensely proud of their brand and quite willing to provide you with some basic information. They will also give you the name of a contact at the network's head office for follow-up.

Visit dedicated websites

The Internet is an excellent source for franchise opportunities, with two sites standing out:

▶ *The BFA's website – www.thebfa.org.uk – lists opportunities offered by their members.*
▶ *Another rich source for franchise leads is the website www.whichfranchise.com; originating in the UK, it offers local content for a growing number of countries. You can search the listings using different search criteria, for example by industry sector, location or investment level. This site offers regional listings, master franchisor opportunities and established franchised business for resale.*
▶ *Several other websites are worth a visit – see Chapter 7 for details.*

Visit franchise exhibitions

Franchise exhibitions are presented at different locations around the UK and internationally throughout the year.

▶ *At least six credible franchise exhibitions take place in various cities throughout the UK – www.franinfo.co.uk has the details.*
▶ *Each one of these exhibitions attracts a large number of sound franchise opportunities under one roof. Workshops on topics related to franchising add to the value proposition and turn a visit into a day well spent.*

Visit small business exhibitions

You can scan general exhibitions and small business exhibitions for franchise leads. Just be extra careful if you follow up on an opportunity that is offered by a non-member of the national franchise association in your country. Why is this important?

I have stressed repeatedly that in most countries around the world, members of their national franchise association are bound by a Code of Ethics for Franchising or similar document. These codes are intended to promote ethics in franchising. Outside the United States, where they have stringent franchise legislation in place, a national association's code is often the only protection a prospective franchisee can obtain.

Copyright issues prevent us from publishing the BFA's Code of Ethics in Franchising. However, the document headed 'Recommended best practices' tells you everything you need to know about ethical franchising. You will find it in Appendix 2 and I urge you to study it carefully before you commence your search for the opportunity of your dreams.

Tip

Most national franchise associations publish their code of ethics on their website. Chapter 7 contains a list of some relevant web addresses.

The pre-selection process

At the beginning of this chapter, I mentioned that I would provide you with several questionnaires. The time has now come to introduce you to the first of them. Due to space constraints, it's not an actual questionnaire, rather, I provide you with a list of questions you need to answer (see pages 130–131). I would advise you to create a proper questionnaire based on the questions I have listed, add whatever is important to you and save the resulting data file as a master file, named, for example, 'Questionnaire 1'.

As you move forward with your investigation of franchise opportunities, you can call up the master file, personalize it for the opportunity on hand and save it as a data file under the name of the specific opportunity. Before long, you will have built up a useful database of franchise opportunities, all laid out in the same way. This will help you to compare 'apples with apples' and home in on the ones that appeal most.

How to pre-select viable franchise opportunities

► *Contact information*
  ▷ *Company name:*
  ▷ *Address:*
  ▷ *Contact person:*
  ▷ *Telephone:*
  ▷ *Email:*
► *Industry sector information*
  ▷ *Type of business/nature of product:*
  ▷ *What appeals to me about this particular franchise?*
  ▷ *What do I imagine I would actually be doing on a daily basis if I were to invest in it?*
  ▷ *Does the investment bracket appear to be within my range?*
  ▷ *Would the business suit my personality?*
  ▷ *Do I have the necessary aptitude to operate this type of business?*
  ▷ *Will I be able to develop a passion for this type of business?*
  ▷ *Could I see myself doing this for a very long time, say a minimum of seven to ten years into the future?*
► *Additional pre-qualifying questions*
  ▷ *Did the company respond promptly to my request for a franchisee information pack?*
  ▷ *Is the material they sent me comprehensive and professionally presented?*
  ▷ *Is the company's website well designed and maintained?*
  ▷ *What have I heard about the company; do they appear to be respected players in their sector?*
  ▷ *Do they do much advertising?*
  ▷ *What do their customers have to say about them?*
  ▷ *Does the product or service appear to be well entrenched in the market?*
  ▷ *Does it seem that the demand for the product is growing?*
  ▷ *What is the competition like?*
► *The potential opportunity*
  ▷ *Do they have an outlet in my neighbourhood?*
  ▷ *If so, does it appear to be busy most of the time?*

> ▷ If there is an outlet already established in my immediate
> surroundings, does this mean that I would have to move
> elsewhere to operate another?
> ▷ Would I be happy to do that?
> ▷ If there is no outlet in the vicinity from where I want to
> trade, is there a viable market for the service?
> ► The way forward
> ▷ Appointment arranged for (date and time) with (name).
> ► Notes

Insight

In my consulting practice, I often meet individuals who have
acquired a franchise from a business that does well at one
location. I explain to them that although a high-class fashion
store rings up record sales in an upmarket shopping centre, it
may not do well at all in a suburban location.

The need for passion

I cannot repeat too often that when you examine the viability of
a franchise opportunity, you should not be guided by its potential
profitability alone. To ensure, as far as this is possible, that
you achieve success in the long term, you need to focus on an
opportunity that you can operate with passion.

Important note!

A survey into the success or otherwise of franchisees selected
from across a wide spectrum of industries revealed that
those who had invested in a particular sector because of its
reputation for profitability but lacked passion for the product
or service produced poor results. Sales figures and profits
tended to lag behind network-wide averages and no amount
of franchisor support could change this. These hapless
franchisees were quick to blame the brand, or the territory.
Their argument did not hold water, however, because as soon
as the units were sold to individuals with a passion for the
product, results improved dramatically.

The evaluation process

As soon as you have a shortlist, the fun really starts. Rank the franchisors of your choice in order of their perceived appeal. This is an arbitrary ranking, reflecting your personal likes and dislikes, so don't sweat over it. As soon as you have set priorities, set up initial meetings with the first two or three franchisors on the list. Remember that although loyalty is an admirable quality, and in fact essential for good franchisor–franchisee relations, it would be premature at this stage. The mere fact that you hit it off with a franchisor representative at a franchise exhibition should not stop you from exploring other options.

THE INITIAL APPROACH

▶ *The franchisee information kit the franchisor will have sent you should have contained an application form. Alternatively, they might email you one on request or have a response page on their website.*
  ▷ *Whatever the medium, take your time to read the instructions carefully before you complete the form. Then write your answers down neatly, comprehensively and above all, truthfully.*
  ▷ *Be especially careful not to overstate your level of experience, or your financial capabilities. The franchisor will undertake a background check and if the resulting findings don't tally with the statements you made in the initial application form, it will count against you.*
  ▷ *Some franchisors want you to return the form either by email, fax or ordinary mail; others prefer that you bring it with you to the first meeting. Just follow their instructions.*
▶ *Arrange an initial 'get-to-know-each-other' session with two or three franchisors of your choice.*

During the first meeting, the onus will be on you to sell yourself to them. This means that you should prepare properly. Depending on practicalities, visit a few of their outlets or at least study their corporate website. Pay particular attention to their corporate history and familiarize yourself with their product range. No need to go overboard, but you will want to make a good impression during your first visit. Some knowledge of the company, its vision and its mission will help you to achieve that.

You should not expect the initial meeting to lead to a firm outcome. Even if it goes extremely well, it is unlikely to create more than an affirmation of mutual interest in principle. Discuss whether the territory of your choice would be available, ask for an estimate of the total investment required and try to get a better understanding of the industry.

Caution advised!

Any attempt by a franchisor to pressurize you into making a binding decision at this stage or, worse still, to ask you for any form of payment should set alarm bells ringing. Professional franchisors are as eager as you are to ensure a perfect match. They know that this takes time and effort from both sides.

FOLLOW-UP

Having visited a reasonable number of franchisors, you will begin to form an impression of which opportunities are worth following up on. The time has come to whittle down your shortlist further and set up subsequent appointments with one or two distinct possibilities. During this next visit, the time is right to pull out the next questionnaire you will have prepared. The following questionnaire provides guidelines for the creation of this document (see pages 134–141). If you applied your mind properly to this task, the questionnaire will have evolved into a substantial document, and yes, it will take some time to complete.

Don't let this worry you; just remember that it is your future that is at stake. You need to base your decision on facts rather than advertising hype and wishful thinking. The franchisor representative knows that and will be happy to oblige. Experience will have taught him that those individuals who do not ask any questions at this stage and just want to sign the franchise agreement spell trouble in the end. Having entered into the deal wearing rose-tinted glasses, they will be quick to complain if at a later stage, something fails to measure up to their perhaps totally unrealistic expectations.

I have compiled the menu of questions to cover all bases. Given your particular circumstances, and the nature of the sector you plan to enter, some questions may lack relevance. Select those that will help you to make an informed decision, and add others you consider relevant. The answers to some questions may be contained in the documentation you have received, or will be contained in brand's disclosure document. Because this tends to vary from one franchise to the next, it is a good idea to work through the questionnaire before your meeting with the franchisor and delete questions that have already been answered. However, you should ask for clarification of any point that remains unclear – there is no such thing as a stupid question!

Questions to ask the franchisor

▶ *Background information*
  ▷ *When was your company established?*
  ▷ *Who are your shareholders?*
  ▷ *Who are your directors?*
  ▷ *Have your company and/or its directors in their personal capacity, encountered debt, criminal or civil proceedings of a material nature, either within the past five years or currently pending?*
▶ *Pilot testing*
  ▷ *How many units of the business you are franchising did the company operate before franchising commenced?*
  ▷ *Where were these units located?*
  ▷ *Did they produce reasonable profits?*
▶ *Franchising*
  ▷ *When did you commence franchising?*
  ▷ *How did you prepare for this important step?*
  ▷ *Has your intellectual property package been legally protected?*

> ▷ How many units do you operate at present?
> ▷ How many of these are franchised?
> ▷ If you no longer operate company-owned units:
>> ▷ Where do you carry out practical franchisee training?
>> ▷ How do you keep in touch with your customers?
>> ▷ Where do you undertake ongoing product and systems development?

► The product or service
> ▷ Is the product new or does it have an established market?
> ▷ If your product or service is based on a successful overseas concept, how did you establish its local market appeal?
> ▷ Is the product protected through patents? If so, who owns these patents?
> ▷ Do you have a formal process for ongoing product development in place?
> ▷ Is the supply of parts/raw materials required to produce the product secured?
> ▷ Are alternative sources of supply available should problems arise? (If one factory is the sole source of supply, a fire or a strike could put the network out of business.)
> ▷ If you are the supplier of the product, or prescribe the supplier:
>> ▷ Under what circumstances would I be allowed to purchase from other sources?
>> ▷ How can I be sure that to purchase from a prescribed source will not erode my profitability?

► The market
> ▷ Is the market for the network's core product growing, stable or in decline?
> ▷ What is your network's current market share?
> ▷ What plans do you have in place to grow it?
> ▷ Who are your major competitors and what is the respective market share each one of them holds?
> ▷ Is the business seasonal?
> ▷ If so, what happens outside seasons?

► *Financial aspects*
  ▷ *How much is the total investment amount and what does it buy me?*
  ▷ *What percentage can be financed?*
  ▷ *Will you assist me in obtaining finance – in what way?*
  ▷ *How much is the upfront fee and what does it buy me?*
  ▷ *What is the total capital cost (equipment, furniture and fittings)?*
  ▷ *What other expenses can I expect to incur during the initial period?*
  ▷ *What happens if your estimates fail to cover the real cost?*
  ▷ *How much working capital do I need?*
  ▷ *How soon will I have to invest additional capital?*
  ▷ *Financial projections for the first three years of operations:*
    ▷ *Will you provide me with sales projections?*
    ▷ *Are these projections based on the demographics of the territory under negotiation, or merely examples loosely based on what others have achieved?*
    ▷ *If the projections are based on another territory, what is their relevance to my territory?*
  ▷ *At what level can I expect to reach breakeven point?*
  ▷ *Are you prepared to provide me with a set of actual trading results of a comparable unit (even if the location is obliterated to protect confidentiality)?*
  ▷ *Ongoing fees:*
    ▷ *How much is your management services fee, how is it calculated and when is it payable?*
    ▷ *Is the fee subject to a minimum fixed payment?*
    ▷ *Does the fee percentage decrease once I exceed a predetermined level of sales?*
  ▷ *Will I be required to contribute to a marketing or advertising fund?*
  ▷ *If so, how is the fee set?*
  ▷ *Am I obliged to spend additional monies on local advertising?*
  ▷ *If so, how much and how is this administered?*

- ▷ If I am obliged to purchase goods from you or a prescribed supplier, do I have to purchase a minimum amount, be it in units of product or monetary terms, each month?
- ▷ Do you levy any other periodic or ongoing fees?
- ▷ If so, what do I get in return?
- ▷ How are these fees calculated and administered?
- ► Legal aspects
  - ▷ Do you provide serious prospects with a disclosure document?
  - ▷ Am I permitted to show the documentation you will provide me with to my professional advisers?
  - ▷ Are you prepared to meet with them, should they request this?
  - ▷ Will I be required to sign a 'confidentiality undertaking' before I receive your confidential documentation?
  - ▷ If so, may I have a copy now so that I can review it at my leisure?
  - ▷ May I have a copy of your franchise agreement?
  - ▷ Is your franchise agreement negotiable or is it absolutely cast in stone?
  - ▷ What is the franchise agreement's initial term?
  - ▷ Is this linked to an option to renew and if so, what are the terms?
  - ▷ Will I be expected to pay a deposit or option fee?
  - ▷ If so, what are the terms?
  - ▷ Under what conditions is it refundable?
  - ▷ Do you offer territorial protection?
  - ▷ Am I subject to territorial constraints of any kind?
  - ▷ Do I have the right to sell my unit at any time?
  - ▷ What restrictions, if any, apply?
  - ▷ Will the purchaser of my unit have to be approved by you and pay an upfront fee?
  - ▷ Would possible restrictions apply even if I wish to pass the unit on to my lawful heirs? If so, please elaborate.
  - ▷ Am I permitted to entrust the day-to-day running of my unit to a manager?
  - ▷ If so, what conditions would be attached to this?

▷ While your franchisee, would I be allowed to operate another (non-competing) business?

▷ Does the franchise agreement contain restraints that endure beyond the period of the agreement and if so, what does this entail?

▷ Does the franchise agreement permit me to add extra items to the standard product range if proven demand exists in my area?

▷ If so, what conditions would apply?

▶ The franchise operation

▷ Are you a member of the national franchise association? (In the UK, for example, this would be the BFA.) If not, why not?

▷ Do you operate a formal franchisee support infrastructure?

▷ How many members of your staff are dedicated to franchisee support?

▷ Will I be able to meet those individuals?

▷ Does your network have an active Franchisee Representative Committee or similar body? If so, who is its chair and may I meet with him or her?

▷ During the past three years, how many franchised units have you:

▷ Established as company-owned branches?

▷ Established under franchise?

▷ Closed down or the franchise agreements cancelled?

▷ Re-purchased from franchisees?

▷ Re-franchised to new franchisees?

▷ During the next three years:

▷ How many units do you intend to establish?

▷ Where will these units be located?

▷ How many of these units will be franchised?

▷ How will your franchisee support infrastructure cope with this planned expansion?

▶ Initial franchisee support

▷ Will you help me with site selection?

▷ Will you advise me regarding the terms of the lease and help me with lease negotiations?

$\triangleright$ Will you supply detailed specifications for the fitting-out of the unit?

$\triangleright$ Am I compelled to use your contractors, or can I choose my own?

$\triangleright$ Is the opening of the unit subject to your formal approval of all equipment and installations?

$\triangleright$ Do you provide initial training and if so, what does this entail?

$\triangleright$ Will my key staff be compelled to attend this training and if so, what does this entail?

$\triangleright$ What costs that are not covered in the original projections will I incur in this regard?

$\triangleright$ Will you assist me with staff selection and if so, to what extent?

$\triangleright$ Will you arrange a 'grand opening' for my unit? If so, what does this entail and what will the cost implications be?

$\triangleright$ Will you help me with the necessary registrations, etc.?

▶ Ongoing franchisee support

$\triangleright$ Will I receive a detailed operations and procedures manual?

$\triangleright$ If so, when has it last been updated?

$\triangleright$ Do you have a programme in place that ensures that it is regularly updated in future?

$\triangleright$ Do you make regular visits to franchisees' units?

$\triangleright$ If so, at what frequency and what does this entail?

$\triangleright$ Do you provide regular ongoing training?

$\triangleright$ If so, what does it entail?

$\triangleright$ Will you train me in 'train the trainer' skills so that I can deliver ongoing staff training?

$\triangleright$ Do you encourage informal interaction among franchisees and if so, how?

$\triangleright$ Do you arrange regular regional and/or national meetings of franchisees?

$\triangleright$ If so, what does this entail?

$\triangleright$ Is participation voluntary or compulsory?

$\triangleright$ What are the cost implications?

▷ Do you have a formal internal communications infrastructure in place, for example planned emails and phone calls, internal newsletters and similar activities?

▷ Do you operate an emergency hotline to help me solve unexpected operational problems?

▷ If so, how does this work?

▷ Are there any extra costs involved?

▷ How do you help franchisees to cope with emergencies, for example prolonged illness or annual leave?

▷ Does the network employ relief managers?

▷ If so, what are the cost implications of using this service?

▶ *Marketing*

▷ Do you have a formal promotional programme in place?

▷ If so, do franchisees have any say in preparing it?

▷ What format does franchisee input take?

▷ If additional local advertising, carried out at my own expense, is either compulsory or necessary, would this be subject to any restrictions?

▷ Do you have a formal programme of ongoing market research in place?

▷ If so, how are the results disseminated to franchisees?

▶ *Summing up*

▷ Are you the original franchisor or are you a sub-franchisor/area developer? If the latter is the case, I will require full details, please.

▷ Would you explain how you established the viability of my proposed territory?

▷ What happens if your assumptions were wrong and it turns out that the site is not viable?

▷ May I spend a day, or a few days, at one of your established units so that I can get a good feel for the business, and what it is really all about?

▷ If you cannot provide me with an up-to-date disclosure document, are you prepared to let me have a letter from:

▷ Your company's auditor confirming that your business is a going concern, likely to be able to meet its ongoing obligations for the foreseeable future?

> ▷ *An officer of your company stating that the company is viable and financially sound?*
> ▷ *May I approach your company's bankers for a reference?*
> ▷ *Assuming we come to a deal:*
>> ▷ *What is the next step?*
>> ▷ *When could I expect to be operational?*
> ▷ *Following the successful operation of my unit over a reasonable period, what would my future expansion possibilities be, for example:*
>> ▷ *Do you offer options over adjacent territories?*
>> ▷ *Would I be permitted to establish additional units within my territory?*
>> ▷ *Would I be permitted to purchase existing units from other franchisees?*
>> ▷ *If so, what conditions, if any, would apply?*

Should the franchisor representative be evasive in his or her response to your questions, or should their response to a request to have a clause in the franchise agreement explained with a response along the lines of: 'it's just legal jargon, don't worry about it', alarm bells should ring again. Such a response could indicate that the franchisor has something to hide, or cares more about making a quick deal than about building a relationship intended to stand the test of time.

Rhetorical questions along the lines of 'don't you trust me?' or 'do you really think I would do that to you?' are either meaningless or another early warning sign that everything is not as it should be. No matter how trustworthy the franchisor representative may be, he or she should know that in a legal sense, you are not dealing with him or her but with the franchisor. In most instances, the franchisor is a registered legal entity. This means that even if you negotiate directly with the owner of the franchise, he or she nevertheless acts as a representative of the franchisor (the franchisor company).

The franchise agreement you will be asked to sign will be between the franchisor (the company) and yourself. There is no telling when this company might be sold, or absorbed into a larger network. Should this happen, the new franchisor representative is not bound by anything his or her predecessor may have offered verbally. There is only one way to ensure the validity of whatever it is you agree on, and this is to have it written into the franchise agreement, or a formal amendment to the franchise agreement.

You should work through the questionnaire with your franchisor paragraph by paragraph, even though this might take more than one session. This will give you valuable insights into the company's standing and approach to franchising.

Tip

Franchise experts often compare a franchise arrangement to a marriage. Now, just like in a marriage the honeymoon is the easy part. Should difficulties arise, they tend to pop up at a later stage. And should things go wrong, you will soon discover that a divorce is often painful, always extremely expensive. A comprehensive franchise agreement is an excellent insurance policy. Make sure you read it and you understand it completely, every single clause of it, before you sign it!

TALK TO EXISTING FRANCHISEES

You should absolutely insist on meeting a good number of the established franchisees, on your terms and without a chaperone in the form of a franchisor representative. Once the franchisor representative has identified you as a serious prospect, and provided he or she has nothing to hide, they will be willing to let you have a list of all franchisees, not just a select few.

Select a few franchisees at random, set up an appointment with them and visit them at their unit. Making appointments is vital because most franchisees are busy people. To gain their full attention requires them to set time aside. Keep in mind, too, that some information is simply too confidential to be shared with a stranger. That said, as long as you ask the right questions and listen carefully to the answers, you will at least walk away with a sound understanding of what it's really like to be a member of the network.

You will find a selection of questions you might want to ask franchisees in the next questionnaire. Use them to create your own questionnaire (see below). The answers you receive (or perhaps do not receive) will tell you a lot about the real state of affairs within the network.

Questions to ask franchisees within the network

Brand, location of the outlet and date of visit
Name of franchisee and contact details

▶ *How long have you been in this business?*
▶ *Did you have prior experience in this sector, or merely a fascination with its workings?*
  ▷ *Would you say that overall, this is a good business to be in?*
▶ *Did you find that broadly speaking the franchisor's initial financial projections were realistic?*
▶ *Is the profitability of your unit in line with financial projections, better or worse than expected?*
▶ *Are you obliged to purchase goods from the franchisor, or a supplier prescribed by the franchisor?*
  ▷ *Do you receive a special deal from the prescribed supplier or could you purchase identical goods for less on the open market?*
▶ *Do you believe that the brand helps you to build your business?*
  ▷ *Would you say that the franchisor does enough to build the brand?*
▶ *Do you get as much support from head office as you were promised you would?*
  ▷ *Do they behave like police officers, or are they really quite helpful?*
▶ *What is the competition in this sector like?*
  ▷ *Does the franchisor generally manage to come up with a viable plan to help you cope with competitor activity?*
  ▷ *Would you say that the network's brand ranks among the top three contenders in the sector?*
▶ *Does the network operate a Franchisee Representative Committee (FRC) or similar body?*

▷ *Do you find its activities useful or do you see it as a mere talk shop?*

▷ *Do you personally hold office within its structures?*

▷ *Do you participate in its activities?*

▶ *Outside the FRC, do you have much interaction with other franchisees in the network?*

▷ *Would you say that franchisees are generally supportive of each other?*

▶ *Does the network organize regional and/or national meetings?*

▷ *If so, what intervals and how often do you attend?*

▷ *Do you find these meetings useful and do you think that the franchisor really listens to franchisees' concerns?*

▶ *Given a chance, would you open additional units of the same brand or is this not as easy as it sounds?*

▶ *If you had a second chance to decide whether you want to join this particular network, what would your decision be?*

Insight

Having worked with many different networks, I have found that there is no need for concern if one or two franchisees appear to be less than enthusiastic about the brand or the sector. Some people like to complain and perhaps they themselves are the problem. Should a pattern of negativity emerge, however, you might wish to look elsewhere.

The way franchisees relate information is also a good indication of the spirit that prevails within the network. If they use the word 'we' a lot and display obvious pride in their brand, it is a good indication that the network is alive, well and going places.

As soon as you have checked out the franchisor and obtained feedback from several franchisees within the network, you will be in a much better position to decide whether you want to link your fortune to that of the network. Once you have made this decision, you need to erase all other opportunities from your mind and focus on the one you have selected. Your franchisor will expect nothing less of you, and your success depends on it.

IT'S A TWO-WAY STREET

At this point, I need to remind you that the franchise relationship is a two-way street. Just like you will want to check out the franchisor's credentials, and are fully within your rights to do so, the franchisor will want to do the same. Allow the franchisor representative to give you a good grilling – it is in your best interest. Why do I say that?

▶ *The characteristics of the business might cause you to become the proverbial square peg in a round hole. This would not be a reflection on your abilities, but if the opportunity is not right for you, you'd better find out before you invest in it.*
▶ *The franchisor may be more interested in collecting upfront fees than in ensuring the long-term success of the network's core business.*
▶ *If the franchisor is less than circumspect in investigating your bona fides, chances are that other applicants are admitted in a similar fashion. This should worry you no end, because the odd rotten apple is bound to slip through the net. In a well-structured network, this will be dealt with swiftly and decisively. But what if the initial investigation of prospects' backgrounds is less than thorough?*

This could lead to a situation where a large number of franchisees have been accepted into the network on the strength of their willingness to put up the investment rather than on their ability to build their unit of the network into the best of its kind in the territory. This could do serious damage to the brand. It would also impact negatively on the standing of your own business, its growth over time and its eventual resale value.

NEXT STEP: A TRIAL MARRIAGE

Congratulations, you are almost there! If, after checking each other out, you and the franchisor remain committed, the time has come to move beyond the courting stage. Roll up your sleeves and enter the trenches. You will work for a few days in one of the network's company-owned stores. The purpose of this exercise is twofold:

▶ *You will experience first hand what your future working life would be like should you go ahead with the project – warts and all.*

▶ *Throughout this period, the franchisor will observe you keenly to assess how you conduct yourself in the trenches – also warts and all!*

Most leading franchisors insist on this trial period and quite clearly, this is in mutual interest. However, the franchisor is about to admit you into the inner sanctum of its enterprise and will want to be assured, firstly, that you are not merely browsing, secondly, that the information you become privy to does not end up in the wrong hands.

ENTERING INTO A PROVISIONAL AGREEMENT

The franchisor may ask you to pay a deposit, and will certainly insist that you sign a confidentiality agreement.

I would advise you to insist that any monies you are asked to pay before the franchise agreement has been signed, for example a deposit, are subject to a pre-agreement and paid into a solicitor's trust account. The agreement dealing with the deposit issue should clearly state the following:

▶ *What is the purpose of making the payment and what is the amount payable?*

▶ *Under what circumstances will the deposit become refundable?*

▶ *Will you receive a full refund, or will a portion go to the franchisor to defray expenses?*

▶ *Which events trigger your right to withdraw from the deal, and what procedure do you have to follow to obtain a refund?*

Example: You are keen to obtain a high street retail franchise but the franchisor does not have a suitable site available. To show that you are serious, you offer to pay a deposit of £10 000. The agreement covering this arrangement should say something along the following lines: 'If no suitable site can be found within 180 days after the deposit has been paid, the franchisee is entitled but not obliged to withdraw from the arrangement and request a refund of X per cent of the full amount.'

> **Important note**
> Should a prospective franchisee elect to withdraw from the
> agreement at this point, some franchisors, having invested
> time and effort to negotiate with the prospective franchisee
> and on the prospective franchisee's behalf, will insist on
> deducting a pre-determined amount to recoup expenses. This
> is acceptable as long as the amount is reasonable and the
> pre-agreement is clear on this point.

I have dealt with the mechanics of the confidentiality undertaking in Chapter 4. Should you be a little hazy on how it works, I advise you to go back to page 118.

Additional considerations

The guidelines given above are comprehensive but do not cover every possibility. Precisely because franchising is highly adaptable, each industry sector will modify the concept to suit its particular needs. Even the organizational culture prevailing within the network will affect the way the franchise operates. The following paragraphs provide some additional pointers you might find useful.

FRANCHISES COME IN DIFFERENT FLAVOURS

No, I am not talking about the 999 different flavours on offer at the local outlet of your favourite ice cream franchise. Rather, I am referring to the different variants of business format franchising you might come across while searching the market for the right opportunity. To qualify, they should all conform to the basic requirements for ethical franchising as set out throughout this book. The main differences are the territorial coverage and the way the franchise is operated.

Initially, most franchisors expected their franchisees to be hands-on in the true sense of the word. The franchisee was licensed to operate one outlet and expected to focus on it, usually to the exclusion of any other business interests. Then two things happened:

▶ *As franchising came of age, corporate managers became interested. They wanted businesses of their own and liked the concept of franchising but were not too keen to be tied to the counter of one unit.*
▶ *Maturing networks realized that individuals with the necessary drive and the funding required to speed up the growth of a given area could help them to grow exponentially. This led to the emergence of multi-unit franchisees and area developers as explained opposite.*

Legitimate variants of business format franchising

SINGLE-UNIT FRANCHISE

This is the classic franchise format, and continues to be the most popular. It describes a single-unit franchise owned and operated by the franchisee. Some years down the line, the franchisee may be offered an opportunity to acquire additional units. However, this is not reflected in the original agreement and will be the subject of further negotiations.

MULTI-UNIT FRANCHISE

An individual or a company acquires the right to establish a series of franchised units over a predetermined number of years. These units will usually be located within a specified territory, and the franchisee operates them for his or her own account. This method of franchising has two shortcomings:

▶ *The contract prescribes the number of units the franchisee is compelled to establish and by when this must be accomplished. Should the initial units fail to perform as expected, the franchisee might be in the unenviable position of having to establish further units, notwithstanding the fact that this does not make commercial sense.*

► *Should the franchisee be financially stronger than the franchisor, the franchisee might exercise undue influence over the way the network operates. This would be a classic example of the 'tail wags dog' syndrome and has the capacity to damage the brand.*

AREA DEVELOPER

An individual or a company acquires the right to establish one franchise within a specified territory and operate it for his or her own account for some time. Once the concept has been tweaked to optimally suit local conditions and the necessary infrastructure has been put in place, the area developer is entitled to sell sub-franchises to others within the same territory. In other words, within a defined area, the area developer assumes the role of franchisor.

Franchisors often use this format if they lack the infrastructure to support franchisees in far-flung areas. The problem with this approach is that franchise fees have to be split between the franchisor and the area developer, making it difficult for either to generate adequate returns.

SATELLITE FRANCHISE

If a franchisor comes across a site he feels has some potential but does not warrant the establishment of a fully-fledged franchise, a satellite franchise might fit the bill. Under this scenario, the franchisor would offer the site to an existing franchisee active in an adjoining area. The franchisee would own and operate the satellite under a supplementary franchise agreement linked to the existing franchise agreement.

A practical example would be a fast-food outlet that offers a limited menu at the satellite site, for example the canteen at a university nearby. Food is prepared at the main unit and transported to the satellite site. This eliminates the need to purchase expensive equipment; it also reduces manpower requirements.

FRACTIONAL FRANCHISE

A franchise occupies premises within an established business. This method lends itself to the setting up of complementary services, for example a car wash within the forecourt area of a petrol station. This format is sometimes described as 'twinning'.

CONVERSION FRANCHISE
This is essentially a standard franchise arrangement but instead of opening a new unit, the franchisor recruits an established operator active in the same field. The franchisee converts the business to the franchisor's corporate image and uses the networks prescribed systems and procedures.

MASTER LICENCE ARRANGEMENT
A foreign franchisor grants a local individual or company, to be known as the master licensee, franchise rights to the entire country. The licensee assumes the rights and obligations of the franchisor within the territory and shares fee income with its foreign principal.

Insight

People often ask me: 'Which format is the best?' I have no clear-cut answer for them. Each one of these sub-concepts works well as long as proven principles of franchising are adhered to. Market realities will dictate which one of them is best suited under a particular set of circumstances.

WHAT IF THE FRANCHISOR IS NEW?

I have stressed repeatedly that when you evaluate franchises, the franchisor's record of accomplishment is of paramount importance. However, everyone has to start somewhere, so where does this leave new franchisors?

When you evaluate a franchise that is new, you will have to make certain allowances, but there are limits. You have to accept, for example, that with the best will in the world, a new franchisor cannot present you with a list of established franchisees.

That's OK, but it should prompt you to investigate the franchise package even more thoroughly than would otherwise be the case.

Should it emerge, however, that the self-styled franchisor is unable to offer you a tried and tested concept, underpinned by the necessary infrastructure to support its effective transfer to franchisees, no franchise exists. Entrepreneurs hoping to develop their systems with income derived from fee payments they collect from naïve franchisees are pretty close to perpetrating fraud. You would be well advised to stay away from their offerings.

Another point you would have to examine in such an instance would be whether the concept is in fact franchiseable. (The wannabe franchisor may well have an excellent business, but not every business lends itself to expansion through franchising.)

In his writings, internationally renowned franchise guru Martin Mendelsohn puts it bluntly: 'It is irresponsible to seek to establish a franchise by trial and error, and at the risk of the initial franchisees. Initial franchisees do not have as their function the operation of pilot units.'

Tip

Let's assume that you are absolutely smitten by the perceived potential of a concept that has not been sufficiently developed to qualify as a franchise. What should you do? I advise you to enter into a joint venture arrangement rather than a franchise. This would give you more influence over the way the concept evolves. And if your instincts were right and the business is a phenomenal success, you will share not only in the risks but also in the rewards on an equal footing.

WHAT IF THE FRANCHISOR IS AN AREA DEVELOPER?

If, during negotiations, it emerges that your franchisor is an area developer or regional licensee, you need to find out who the contracting party is and who, in the course of day-to-day operations, will be responsible for what.

You should establish, too, what would happen should either the area developer/regional licensee or the franchisor/licensor (the original owner of the rights) go out of business. The same would apply should a local company purchase a master licence for the entire country and act as the local franchisor.

These scenarios are not as farfetched as they may sound; just consider the following:

A grants the development rights for an entire territory to B. B is entitled to grant franchises within the territory, but is obliged to pass a certain percentage of fees he stands to collect on to A. However, B fails to do so, eventually prompting A to cancel the agreement with B. Where does this leave B's franchisees – how are their interests protected?

I am not suggesting that sub-franchise arrangements are inherently flawed. They are a legitimate instrument in franchising but should be examined carefully by an expert. This will ensure that the franchisee's rights are properly protected.

BUYING AN ESTABLISHED FRANCHISE

One route into owning a franchise that is gaining in importance as more and more franchised networks reach maturity is to purchase an established unit, or resale. Should you consider this option, proceed as follows:

► *The first thing you need to establish is how the franchisor feels about the transaction. Although the franchisee owns the business, the franchise agreement will almost certainly stipulate that the franchisor has to approve the sale. It would be unwise to see this as a mere formality.*

▷ Perhaps the franchisor has a right of first refusal and plans to exercise it. If so, you would be wasting your time pursuing the matter further.

▷ Is the franchisor prepared to grant you the franchise? If not, see above.

Insight

I often find that buyers of established franchises consider negotiations with the franchisor to be a mere formality. It is not! For the deal to become valid, the prospective buyer will have to go through the network's evaluation and training process.

▷ The outgoing franchisee's franchise agreement is irrelevant. You need to discuss the franchise agreement with the franchisor; it is usually advisable to enter into a new agreement rather than take over the remaining period in the existing one.

▷ Do you feel comfortable joining this network? You need to be aware that there is no difference between setting up a new unit or acquiring an established one. Once you are a franchisee, you fall under the rules and regulations of the franchise.

▶ Having passed the first hurdle, it is time to find out what the reasons for the resale are. Two likely scenarios come to mind:

▷ The unit could be highly successful. The only reason why the franchisee wants to sell is that he or she wants to retire.

▷ On the other end of the scale, the unit could be barely making it, or even trade at a loss.

Both scenarios offer opportunities but you need to know early on during negotiations what you are dealing with. The franchisor will assist, but you need to do your own due diligence investigation. This calls for the involvement of an expert, be it a business consultant, solicitor or accountant, who has proven expertise in such dealings.

▷ If the unit is trading profitably, you need to balance the advantage of buying a business as a going concern against

> the extra cost in the form of a goodwill payment the
> outgoing franchisee will demand.
>> ▷ If the unit is in bad shape, you need to find out the
>> reasons why this is so and assess whether you can fix
>> it. Quite clearly, the asking price should reflect the true
>> situation.
> ▶ Although the outgoing franchisee might try to tell you
> otherwise, it will be in your best interest to work closely with
> the franchisor.
>> ▷ As soon as the outgoing franchisee has received his or her
>> money, they have no interest whatsoever in the future of
>> the business.
>> ▷ The franchisor, on the other hand, has a vital interest to
>> ensure that once you are on board, business continues at
>> least as before but preferably with added impetus.
>> ▷ One final tip: Do not be content to shadow the outgoing
>> franchisee. Insist on being trained by the franchisor.

There should be no doubt in your mind that your future lies with
the franchisor.

A BRIEF LOOK AT INTERNATIONAL FRANCHISING

Franchising is tailor-made to serve as a vehicle for international
expansion, and a growing number of networks expand
internationally, some with outstanding success. But international
expansion must be tackled for the right reasons, or it can go
horribly wrong. Providing guidelines for international master
licensing would exceed the framework of this book. I have to limit
myself to describing the fundamentals, and caution you not to
become involved in a half-baked venture of this kind.

Experience has shown that it does not make sense to expand
internationally unless:

> ▶ The original operation shows signs of approaching maturity.
> Coverage of the home market is almost complete and
> opportunities for further expansion are limited.

- ▶ *The franchisor has access to adequate resources. As you will see, transplanting a brand into a foreign country requires specialized manpower, money and plenty of patience.*
- ▶ *Target markets should be selected because they show clear synergies. For starters, being able to converse in the same language helps a lot. And if market conditions are similar, things become even easier. But it is never easy – market research must be carried out before the brand is launched.*
- ▶ *The franchisor should be prepared to invest time and effort into building the brand in the target country. This will be expensive, and profits are unlikely to materialize in the short term.*

Foreign expansion can take place in several ways. The most common are to offer master licence rights to a carefully selected individual in the target country, or the franchisor could set up a branch operation that acts as the local franchisor. From then onwards, the steps towards the launch of the franchise are almost the same as those taken when the franchise was originally set up. They involve market research, tweaking of the product and adaptation of the marketing programme to suit the local culture, operation of a pilot outlet and establishment of the franchisee support infrastructure.

To paraphrase franchise guru, Martin Mendelsohn, once more: If you want to expand internationally, start with some projections:

- ▶ *Estimate the time it will take to get the foreign operation up and running, then double it.*
- ▶ *Estimate the investment it will take then double it.*
- ▶ *Estimate how much profit you will earn within the initial three to five years of operations, then half it.*

Some people spend their holidays in a far away land and fall in love with some local product or service. 'This would do well in my home country' they think to themselves and acquire a 'master licence' of sorts. After returning home, they set up the operation and begin selling franchises. This is not how to do it and if you come across such an offer, I advise you to walk away.

THE IMPORTANCE OF PERSONAL CHEMISTRY

Once you have completed your investigation, and no matter how well it pans out, you will have to ask yourself one more question. It is the most difficult of all to answer, and no expert will be able to answer it for you. It is simply this:

'Do I feel comfortable dealing with this particular franchisor and its team – now – in three to five years' time?' This is more important than you might think. After all, for a franchised network to become truly successful and build prosperity for its stakeholders there needs to be ongoing close cooperation between the franchisor and all its franchisees. In other words, the franchise relationship is a perennial give-and-take and it is of vital importance that you get on well with everyone involved.

Insist on meeting the members of the franchisor's team and assess the prevailing organizational climate at the franchisor's head office. You could, for example, ask the franchise manager how long he or she has been with the company. Don't be alarmed if the franchise manager's reply is 'three months'. You need to accept that the franchise sector is on the move and job-hopping is the order of the day.

If, however, you go on to speak with the bookkeeper and the receptionist and the market research assistant and the tea lady and they all are new, it could indicate a serious lack of stability within the franchisor company. There might be a logical explanation for all this but if I were you, I would insist on getting one. Precisely because you will depend on the franchisor's support, and are expected to pay good money for the privilege, stability within the ranks is of great importance to you.

Wrapping it up

If you have a good feeling about the brand and are prepared to join up, review your motives once more. By talking to a variety of franchisees, I gained the distinct impression that those of them who were successful went into business because they wanted to, not because they had to.

This is not to say that individuals who had been retrenched and were unable to secure alternative employment have no hope of succeeding. To become successful, however, they had to make a conscious decision to take charge of their future by joining the ranks of the self-employed.

Many of those who fail as franchisees are former corporate employees who desperately miss the penthouse office, the large car, business class travel and all the other status symbols that went with the job they no longer have. They bitterly resent the fact that they were forced out of the corporate cocoon they thought was secure. They may even consider a career as the owner of a small business to be something that is really beneath them.

And what about those who still have a job but want to operate a business of their own? Exchanging a seemingly secure position for the vagaries of business ownership requires a major leap of faith that should not be undertaken lightly. Those who have done it recommend that you base your decision on:

▶ *Careful soul searching and self-evaluation (what can I do best and am I sure that this is what I want to do for the rest of my life?)*

- ▶ Learning all you can about franchising. The concept works, but if you are not prepared to follow the system's rules, being a franchisee will be hell for you as well as for your franchisor.
- ▶ Thorough research of the available opportunities; it is especially important to speak to established franchisees within the networks you investigate. Without exception, those franchisees I spoke to stated that they would be happy to talk to prospective franchisees and share their experiences with them.
- ▶ Working at a company-owned store before making the final decision. When you look in from the outside, a particular business may look glamorous. However, its attractiveness may not stand up to the grind of a daily routine. For example, many people fancy themselves as witty entertainers and amateur chefs of note. They plough all their money into a restaurant, only to find that the daily grind involves dealing with obnoxious customers, handling staff problems and working crazy hours. Once disillusionment sets in, passion goes out of the window and the business fails.
- ▶ Having enough money to fund the establishment of the business and working capital needs. It is usually better to start a smaller business and build it up slowly than to overextend yourself initially and struggle to make ends meet. This saps your energy and business success may elude you.

'You never achieve real success until you like what you are doing.'

Dale Carnegie

If you followed my guidelines, you will have passed this final review with flying colours. Keep your emotions aside for a little while longer, however, and consider your advisors' comments once more. If everything seems in order, you are ready to sign the franchise agreement, well, almost ready. One more item requiring clarification is how long it will take from the time you sign the franchise agreement and pay over the initial fee to the day your unit will be ready to open its doors for business.

The answer depends on several factors, including your existing commitments and, in business sectors where location is important, the availability of a suitable site. You should, however, insist on a binding commitment. If you are currently employed or operate another business, it would be unwise to leave your job or sell your business, only to sit idly at home. You would be forced to draw on your rapidly dwindling savings while the franchisor hunts for a suitable site.

Should you be unemployed, you might be able to convince the franchisor to let you work as a trainee manager in a company-owned store. The salary won't be much, but it would pay for your living expenses. And you would have the opportunity of a lifetime to learn the business from the bottom up.

Once the agreement has been signed and a site secured, your franchisor will schedule the initial training period. I urge you not to rush this step; rather, allocate as much time as you possibly can to training because extensive practice will increase the confidence you need to operate your own unit successfully.

In course of my work, I came across a document that a very successful franchisor issued to qualified prospects. In my view, it epitomizes the spirit of franchising and it is reproduced below.

A franchisor's pledge

Upon joining my network, you will become my partner in the business. The way I see it, I shall depend on you just as much as you depend on me. Your success will be my success and your gain will be my gain. It is in our mutual interest to help each other as much as possible. You know by now what I expect of you, so it's only fair to tell you, in everyday language and staying clear of legal jargon, what you can expect from me:

INDUCTION AND TRAINING

▶ *The franchise agreement I offer is used throughout the network and conforms to all known principles of ethical franchising.*

▶ *I will train you in the theory and practice of operating the business profitably and to the delight of your customers. Formal initial and ongoing training sessions are planned, but should you feel at any stage that you need additional training, I will be pleased to offer it.*

GETTING YOU READY TO TRADE

▶ *I will render assistance with site selection, lease negotiations and the fitting-out of the premises.*

▶ *For the benefit of the network, I negotiate bulk deals with suppliers but you deal directly with them. I categorically state that I do not receive any financial benefits linked to my franchisees' dealings with prescribed suppliers.*

▶ *I undertake to help you select and train staff to agreed network-wide standards.*

STORE OPENING

▶ *I will provide a comprehensive opening package that has been proven to successfully announce your arrival in your town.*

▶ *I will help you to set up the administrative systems and procedures needed to control operations in the widest sense of the word effectively.*

▶ *I undertake to have a competent person present at your store for the entire first month after opening, at no additional cost to you.*

ONGOING SUPPORT

▶ *I maintain a troubleshooting hotline that is manned 24/7. I undertake that if I cannot help with a business-related problem, I will find someone who can.*

▶ *I will visit your outlet at least once a month to review operations and advise on problems linked to quality or productivity.*

▶ *I promise to respect your status as the owner of the business and any criticism, if called for, will be constructive.*

▶ *Should a competitor affect your ability to operate profitably,*
  I will find out how they do it and introduce appropriate
  counter-measures.
▶ *Whenever you need to discuss something business-related, I*
  will make myself available.

In closing, I could not do better than to quote Greg Nathan,
psychologist and expert in franchisor/franchisee relations. He
defines the real task of the franchisor as:
'Putting people into business and providing them with the
systems and support that enables them to achieve their
personal and financial aspirations.'
I will strive at all times to live up to this pledge and look
forward to welcoming you into my family!
Your franchisor

THE TEN MOST IMPORTANT THINGS YOU NEED TO REMEMBER

1 Procrastination is your enemy no. 1. Regardless of whether the economy is in an upward cycle or on the skids, the best time to make your move is now.

2 Moving ahead does not equate to moving ahead blindly. One of the most important factors in the equation is you. Your likes, dislikes, experiences and professional skills must all be taken into account.

3 Once you know that becoming a franchisee is what you really want to do, potentially for the rest of your life, select a franchise with care. Do not allow yourself to be attracted to a seemingly attractive opportunity like moths are attracted to a light source. Check it out or you might share the moths' fate by getting burned.

4 While it is not a good idea to fall for the first franchise opportunity you come across, the opposite approach is not recommended either. Unless you make a decision within a reasonable period, the warning contained in paragraph 1 applies.

5 When you meet with a franchisor, be yourself. Above all, project a confident image, all the while being mindful of the fact that there is a very thin line between self-confidence and bravado. Don't cross it!

6 Having decided on the industry sector that interests you, you should investigate several brands. Only once you have the feeling that this is the one should you sign a confidentiality undertaking. Granted, a confidentiality undertaking doesn't force you into a binding deal but it could preclude you from following other opportunities within the sector.

7 *Should a franchisor representative spin you a yarn along the line of, 'Someone else is interested in your territory, unless you make up your mind now, you are going to miss out', let it go. Other opportunities will come up but if you commit yourself to the wrong one, it will be difficult and expensive to withdraw.*

8 *The best way of getting the inside story about a network is to talk to several of its existing franchisees. You being a stranger in their eyes, they may not tell you everything they know but their body language will provide valuable clues.*

9 *Working in the business of your dreams for a few weeks before you sign the franchise agreement can be a real eye opener. If given an opportunity to do so, take it with both hands.*

10 *Take it from me, there is no such thing as a 'best franchise'. It's a case of 'horses for courses' – not every concept will perform equally well in different parts of the country, and your abilities, likes and dislikes will play a major role in the eventual success or otherwise of the venture.*

6

What should happen next?

In this chapter you will learn:

- *the extent of initial support you can expect to receive*
- *how to get the best out of the initial training period*
- *the extent of ongoing support you can expect to receive*
- *how you can maximize the value of the franchise*
- *how the franchisee lifecycle concept is likely to affect you*

'The way to get started is to quit talking and begin doing.'

Walt Disney, entertainment pioneer

It's official: The agreement has been signed, the initial fee has been paid and you are now a franchisee. You move around in a bit of a haze, sensing that magical things are happening all around you but you are not quite sure what. You might even feel apprehensive at times, but that's OK too. You have taken a big step and it may need some time before you settle in.

In this chapter, I will take you through the process of settling in as a franchisee as it is likely to unfold. Given the diversity of franchises, things might happen a little differently than I describe them but don't let this worry you. A sound understanding of the principles will help you to face your future with confidence. I will also deal with some peripheral issues of interest to franchisees and franchisors alike, including Greg Nathan's important work around the franchisee lifecycle concept.

Initial support

This is the first real test of the franchise relationship, and it involves both sides:

▶ *As a franchisee, you need to be prepared to focus on the task of building your business and work harder than you have ever worked before in your life. On the upside, you can look forward to extensive initial support from your franchisor. And do not forget, you have become part of a family made up of a group of enthusiastic fellow-franchisees who share your dreams and pull in the same direction. Most of your peers within the network will have gone through the same learning curve you are facing up to right now. Chances are that they will be happy to share their experiences with you.*

▶ *Franchisors need to remember that they have a moral responsibility to guide their franchisees towards business success. Following careful selection of prospects, this involves providing extensive initial and ongoing support and a willingness to literally go the extra mile for each franchisee.*

These factors combine to make the task of building your new business that much easier. A more detailed description of the things the franchisor will do for you on the one hand and expects to get out of the relationship on the other follows.

GETTING THE UNIT READY

▶ *Your franchisor will help with site selection, lease negotiations and the fitting out of the unit. This does not mean that you should stay on the sidelines and watch the franchisor get on with the job. Your money is being spent and you owe it to yourself to stay involved.*

▶ *In case of a turnkey operation, things might be a little different. The franchisor will have selected the site, taken out a head lease and prepared the unit for trading. In this scenario, all you will be expected to do is walk in and start operations. This notwithstanding, it is your future that is at stake and you should evaluate key aspects of the proposition. You could, for example, do your own site evaluation. And you definitely need to have the lease contract for the business premises scrutinized by a competent solicitor, even though you may be sub-leasing from the franchisor.*

Insight

I have personally witnessed many instances when new franchisees made a nuisance of themselves by questioning the wisdom of the development team's every move. Keep informed about the way your money is being spent but also respect the fact that the franchisor's people are professionals who have done it all many times before.

INTRODUCTORY TRAINING

Having spent a few days at a company-owned store during the evaluation stage, you may be convinced that you have grasped the basic concepts and are ready to start trading, but not so fast. The franchisor will have developed a training programme that has been carefully designed to prepare a novice for every eventuality; I advise you to make full use of it. In fact, if you are offered the chance to spend a few extra days in training, take it with both hands, especially if it involves practical tasks.

While it is possible to deliver the theoretical part of the training course according to a laid-down schedule, hands-on exposure to practical tasks does not always work this way. The more time you spend at a company unit the better your chances of becoming exposed to the full range of tasks you will eventually have to cope with. By learning from your mistakes during training, you are less likely to repeat them once you are on your own.

The following text lists ten pointers for getting the best from the initial training experience. Study them carefully and you will be well prepared.

The smart franchisee's ten guiding principles for training

I am the learner

1 *I accept that only I, being the learner, can learn; with the best will in the world, nobody else can do that for me.*
2 *I know precisely what is expected of me.*
3 *I am motivated to learn because I know that it will have a direct and measurable impact on the success of my own business.*
4 *I am confident that I will be allowed to learn at my own pace, and that nobody will make me feel bad about it.*

Learning material

5 *I know that the learning material I have received is relevant, and will impact directly on the success of my business.*
6 *I accept that the material will be presented in optimal size portions but if I fall behind, I will not hesitate to speak up.*

Learning techniques

7 *I know that I learn best if I apply in practice what I have learnt. For this reason, I am willing to do anything, no matter how simple.*
8 *I welcome the feedback I receive from my trainer.*
9 *No matter how simple the task, I know and accept that only repetition will make me perfect.*
10 *I understand that practice in a variety of settings will enhance my ability to absorb new concepts and apply them in practice.*

PRE-OPENING PROCESS

COMMISSIONING THE UNIT

The franchisor representative will check and recheck everything to make sure that the unit conforms to the network's corporate identity guidelines. He or she will also test the equipment, check opening stock and make sure that all systems are up and running.

Some franchisors do that while you attend training. Should your training course be completed, however, spending time shadowing this person will be time well spent.

▶ *It will increase your understanding of the processes involved.*
▶ *You will get to know some of the people you will deal with in future, for example the technicians who will initially install and subsequently maintain your equipment.*

HIRING STAFF

In most instances, staff will have to be hired and trained and the franchisor will help you with that.

▶ *Key staff members might need to participate in some of the training sessions you attend.*
▶ *Others will be trained to prepare and/or deliver the product or service in keeping with the network's systems and procedures.*

OPENING CAMPAIGN

At this stage, the franchisor is likely to set an opening campaign in motion. This will ensure that the day your unit opens for business, people will be aware of your presence. The format of the campaign will vary widely depending on the business sector you are in.

▶ *The franchisor will know from experience what is likely to work best and that should guide you.*
▶ *Keep in mind that unless the cost of the campaign is built into the initial fee, you will have to foot the bill. This should not come as a surprise as it will have been allowed for in the financial projections.*

INITIAL HAND-HOLDING

For a few days after the opening of your business, a franchisor representative is likely to be at hand to offer moral and practical support. Some franchisors even make a dedicated start-up team available. This is a group of highly experienced operators drawn from their company-owned units. They spend a few days with your staff to ensure that everything functions like clockwork. On the opening day and for a couple of days thereafter, they will perform your staffs' functions hands-on, shadowed by your own people. After a gradual role reversal, your team will take over and the franchisor's people will withdraw.

> **Tip**
> Don't be intimidated by the apparent complexity of the opening process. Your franchisor will have a series of checklists detailing everything that needs to be done, who will do it and by when it needs to be completed.

Support continues indefinitely

The mere fact that your business is finally up and running should not mean that your franchisor's support activities come to a grinding halt. Ongoing support is a hallmark of professional franchising, but this cannot be a one-way street. It is up to you to make use of the programmes the franchisor makes available, and if you need help in an area that is not covered by the formal support programme, you should not be shy to ask.

But there are limits. Some franchisees expect their franchisor to do everything for them. Commercial realities dictate that this is not sustainable. A franchisor who attempts to operate a franchisees' businesses in exchange for a very limited return, namely the franchise fee, would soon go out of business. Operational aspects are your responsibility, and this includes building the potential of your business at local level. Access to the franchisor's programmes will ease the burden quite considerably for you.

NATIONAL BRAND BUILDING

To market the brand effectively ranks high among the franchisor's ongoing responsibilities. Examples of areas this involves follow.

MARKET RESEARCH

The franchisor will coordinate network-wide efforts to keep abreast of market trends.

PRODUCT DEVELOPMENT

The franchisor will develop new products, and tweak existing ones to ensure that the network's offering stays ahead of that of competitors.

▶ *In the interest of brand uniformity, franchised networks like to present a cohesive range of products and/or services. For this reason, most franchisors frown upon franchisees initiating changes to the product range without discussing this with the Field Service Consultant (FSC) first.*

▶ *Should you come across an item you think will sell well at your store, raise the idea with your FSC. He or she will pass it on through the correct channels where it will be treated like a new product idea.*

▶ *Following a period of testing, and subject to market response, the product will be introduced throughout the network. However, you will be recognized as the originator of the idea. Subject to the idea's market potential, this might even earn you a placing in the network's annual franchisee awards.*

YOUR CONTRIBUTION

The most important contribution you can make towards growing the brand and with it your business is to literally live the brand. For example:

▶ *Deliver on the implied promise of the network's national marketing campaigns. Should a campaign revolve around a product promotion, for example, it is your task to stock the range on promotion in sufficient quantities. Few things annoy customers more than if they take the trouble to respond to an advertising message only to be told that the item on promotion is out of stock.*

▶ *Link your local marketing efforts to the national theme; your franchisor may have materials available that help you to get the message across at store level.*

► You will find that your franchisor will be protective of the brand and the way it is presented to the public. It is in your interest as well as in the interest of the network that your campaigns comply fully with corporate identity guidelines. Research has shown that even the smallest deviation from approved standards can weaken brand identity. For this reason, your franchisor will insist on approving every campaign before you implement it, and you should not resent that.

► Keep your eyes and ears open. Being at the network's frontline, you can talk to customers and find, for example, what, if anything, they would like differently. And if you become aware of something the competition is up to, investigate it thoroughly.

► By communicating your findings to the franchisor, you can help, firstly, to develop better products and, secondly, to sharpen the network's responses to competitor activity. As a member of the network, you win as well – just one example of a win–win situation that is a hallmark of professional franchising.

NETWORK-WIDE PURCHASING PROGRAMME

This is another pillar of the franchise arrangement. If operating the franchise involves selling a product, or purchasing inputs for the performance of a service, your franchisor will either act as the supplier or negotiate preferential deals with third-party suppliers. This makes perfect sense because the combined buying power of all members of the network will ensure that everyone receives a better deal.

Most franchisees, if asked what they value most in the franchise relationship, will place 'access to bulk purchase arrangements' on top of their lists. Commercial realities dictate, however, that this advantage comes with an obligation.

To gain access to preferential pricing, the franchisor needs to convince suppliers that the network's combined purchases will amount to an agreed minimum quantity. To deliver on this promise, the franchisor has no option but to compel all franchisees to participate. It follows that if your brother in law offers you a special deal on a product you would otherwise purchase from a prescribed source, but the deal is not accessible to other members of the network, you might have to pass.

Similar considerations would apply to joint marketing drives. The more members of the network participate the higher the effectiveness of the campaign can be expected to be.

THE FIELD SERVICE CONSULTANT'S ROLE

Expect a Field Service Consultant to call at your unit at regular intervals. Some franchisees make the mistake of seeing this individual as a police officer, sent by the franchisor to catch them doing something wrong. Nothing could be further from the truth. In every enlightened network, the FSC's main role is to help franchisees to improve the profitability of their businesses.

Granted, this will involve checking that the network's systems and procedures are effectively implemented, and the corporate identity is kept intact. This is in your own best interest, however, because it impacts directly on the way your business performs.

FREE FLOW OF IDEAS

The life of an independent entrepreneur can be lonely at times, and this is where franchising really comes to the fore. In addition to regular store visits by your FSC, you can look forward to regional and national meetings. And someone should always be prepared to listen and, at the very least, make constructive suggestions, should a franchisee need help, or simply a shoulder to cry on.

Expansion opportunities for franchisees

During the early days in the development of franchising, franchisors generally resented the idea of having one franchisee own more than one unit. More recently, most franchisors not only allow franchisees to own more than one unit but actually encourage this. In my book, the wisdom of this practice can be debatable and I would advise you to consider its pros and cons before you join a network that allows it.

On the face of it, the concept of multiple-unit franchise ownership goes against one of the core principles of franchising, namely that the franchise owner manages the unit hands-on. If a franchisee controls more than one unit, managers will have to be entrusted with day-to-day operations. In some instances, this can cause problems; in others, the practice works extremely well. A franchisee of a national chain of motor spares stores related his experience to me – see below:

A franchisee's experience

After I had achieved excellent results from my first outlet, I opened up a further two. My plan was to continue managing one outlet hands-on and delegate day-to-day management of the other two units to salaried managers. Extensive ongoing support by the franchisor, which included weekly visits by head office representatives, notwithstanding, performance of the manager-operated outlets failed to match that of the unit I controlled hands-on.

I first tried to address this by moving from store to store but this did not bring the desired results. The moment I had one unit performing up to scratch and turned my attention on another one, problems that I thought I had successfully addressed would resurface.

In our business, pressure on mark-ups limits the scope for lavish salaries and incentive schemes. This limits the calibre of people I can attract as managers. Eventually, careful evaluation of performance figures convinced me that it would make better commercial sense to focus my attention on one unit and sell off the others.

This I did and already, my original business shows a healthy upward trend. Even more pleasing is the fact that the purchasers of the other two units report solid performances, proof supreme that their full-time presence in their respective businesses is paying handsome dividends.

The above case study notwithstanding, many examples of successful multiple-unit ownership exist. One could say that it is a growing trend. Success depends on several factors, including:

▶ *The industry sector and its profit potential, as this affects the franchisee's ability to offer attractive packages to talented managers.*
▶ *The level of standardization within the business. It is easier for an absentee owner to control a highly standardized operation, for example a fast-food outlet, than one that offers customized products, for example a quick-service print store.*
▶ *The location of the second and subsequent units owned by the same franchisee. It is obviously easier for one individual to control several units if these are clustered together rather than located hundreds of miles apart.*
▶ *The management style of the franchisee. Some franchisees thrive on the responsibility to oversee a number of units; others prefer to focus on one operation in a more hands-on fashion.*

CONSIDERATIONS AROUND CONVERSION FRANCHISING

If you have an existing small business and want to join an established franchise network, don't be blinded just by the joint purchase power of the network and the national brand building activities the franchisor undertakes. The benefits will be there for the taking, but to reap them you must be prepared to embrace the franchisor's systems and willing to become part of a group of like-minded people with similar goals.

How to get the best out of franchising

To get the best out of the franchise arrangement, you need to be pro-active throughout. This means that you should participate in every activity the franchisor arranges for the benefit of franchisees, for example:

▶ *When the Field Service Consultant responsible for your area calls, be cooperative and set aside quality time. This will ensure that you derive the most benefit from the visit.*
▶ *Attend training sessions as well as regional and national meetings. Not only will you learn about developments within the network first-hand, but by mixing with fellow franchisees, you will be able to benefit from their experiences.*
▶ *Make yourself heard. Your franchisor is not a mind reader; so if you need help, ask for it! The old saying, the squeaky wheel gets greased first also comes to mind.*

Selling your franchise

If you are just thinking about entering the exciting world of franchising, the possibility of selling the business at some future date will not feature highly on your list of concerns. You should consider this eventuality nonetheless because the day may come when you want to move on, or retire.

Although as a franchisee, you own the business, your right to sell it will be restricted by a clause in the franchise agreement. This was briefly discussed in Chapter 4 but the importance of this aspect merits an additional explanation.

The actual mechanics of selling your business depend on the clauses dealing with this issue in your franchise agreement. In all likelihood, your franchisor will have reserved the right to assess the potential buyer's profile against the network's franchisee selection criteria as applied at the time of the sale. This is only fair; neither the franchisor nor the other franchisees in the network should be expected to welcome someone into the family who does not meet normal selection criteria.

Some franchisors reserve the right of first refusal to purchase the business from you. This is similar to an option; if it applies, the franchise agreement needs to contain provisions on how it will be dealt with. In most cases, the franchisor will have agreed to pay the highest genuine price you were offered in an arm's length transaction. Alternatively, an independent professional valuator could be called upon to set the price. The important thing is that agreement needs to be reached at the beginning of the relationship, not at the time you are ready to sell.

What if the unthinkable should happen?

Survival rates among new business start-ups are notoriously low. Nobody seems to know for sure how low; many statistics have been bandied about in the past but whenever I quote any of them, someone in the audience jumps up and offers irrefutable proof that this particular statistic has been discredited.

It is safe to say, however, that a franchise offers a significantly higher likelihood of success than an independent business. Provided that you have made the right selection and follow the network's system to the letter, you are unlikely to encounter financial problems. It is equally unlikely that the franchisor's operation should fail. Regardless of how remote this possibility might be, it does exercise some prospective franchisees' minds. For this reason, I will refer briefly to the likely impact of financial distress on franchisees and franchisors alike.

THE FRANCHISEE IN FINANCIAL DISTRESS

Should the spectre of financial distress raise its ugly head, it would be important that you involve the franchisor as early as possible. This is not the time to display false pride. It is much better to explain your situation and ask for help in resolving it. In this context, you need to understand that in a legal sense, the franchisor is probably under no obligation to assist. However, you are trading under the network's brand name and the last thing any franchisor would want is to have the brand linked to financial failure.

What would probably happen is that the franchisor will do a due diligence of your business. Once the origins of the problem have been uncovered, franchisor representatives will work closely with you to plot a viable route to recovery. This might involve a need to refinance the business. Granted, raising finance at that stage may be difficult but it is possible.

▶ *If you come up with a sound plan, and have the franchisor on your side, the bank might be willing to assist with a cash injection.*
▶ *Suppliers might grant you a temporary reprieve, usually on condition that you pay cash for new deliveries and pay off the backlog over an extended period.*

Should you hide your true financial situation from your franchisor and struggle on for as long as possible, things are almost certain to reach a point where recovery is no longer possible. At that stage, the only remaining option would be to sell the unit, but, given the circumstances, don't bet on achieving a favourable price. Even in this situation, however, your chances of recovering some money would be infinitely greater than if you were an independent operator facing liquidation.

THE FRANCHISOR IN FINANCIAL DISTRESS

It is a prerequisite for franchising that the franchisor is financially stable. You will have verified this during your initial investigation of the opportunity. It is possible, though highly unlikely, that a company that was in good financial health at the time you joined the network experiences problems at a later stage. How would this affect you as a franchisee?

> **Insight**
>
> Neither the franchisor nor the franchisees of a network can be held legally responsible for each other's debts. There is absolutely no risk that the franchisor's creditors could come knocking on franchisees' doors to collect the franchisor's debts. This does not necessarily mean that franchisees remain unaffected. Should franchisees owe the franchisor money, its creditors will be ruthless in collecting it; franchisees need to be prepared for that.

From a legal standpoint, should the franchisor be unable to meet its obligations under the franchise agreement, franchisees would probably be entitled to ask a competent court to have the franchise agreement set aside. If, for example, the franchisor is no longer able to offer substantial ongoing support and this state of affairs is likely to continue for an extended period, it would amount to a breach of the franchise agreement.

Under this scenario, former franchisees would probably be able to continue operations as independents or, should they so wish, they could band together and form a new entity. Alternatively, ex-franchisees of a defunct network could acquire the network's intellectual property rights from the liquidator and continue trading. As far as the network's customers and suppliers are concerned, it would be 'business as usual'.

Formal franchisee representation

Throughout this book, I have compared being a member of a franchised network to being a member of a family. Taking this analogy one step further, let me suggest that the fortunes of powerful families are guided by a family patriarch. The patriarch will direct the family's fortunes, but not before listening carefully to advice from members of the family council. In a franchised network, this would be the Franchisee Representative Council (FRC) or similar structure.

Having formal franchisee representation can be highly constructive, as long as the franchisor does not see it as an adversarial body and franchisees do not use it as a whingeing forum. Its real purpose is to serve as a forum for the expression of franchisees' needs, with the objective of strengthening the network as a whole. An informal precedent for this can be found in almost every network. New franchisors tend to consult with every single franchisee before implementing a change in direction. As the network grows, practicalities make this increasingly difficult and that's where a FRC comes into its own. To ensure its credibility, the FRC should:

▶ *Be managed by franchisee representatives elected by their peers;*
▶ *Have its own constitution;*
▶ *Be independently funded, although progressive franchisors will make back-up services available.*

In larger networks, the FRC will consist of a national and several regional structures that meet regularly throughout the year to exchange ideas. After considering franchisees' inputs, the FRC's leadership will meet with the franchisor, discuss concerns of mutual interest and report back to members. Arguably the two most important functions a well-managed FRC fulfils are to:

▶ *Assist the franchisor in setting the network's future direction. Because the FRC's representatives have a mandate from other franchisees and are guided in deliberations by franchisees' wishes, they will find it much easier to 'sell' resulting changes to franchisees.*
▶ *Keep errant franchisees in check. Reckless actions by even one impetuous franchisee can damage the brand. Although the franchisor has an obligation to keep franchisees in check, this can easily develop into an 'us versus them' scenario that does irreparable harm to the relationship. It is much easier for duly mandated FRC representatives to approach the franchisee and point out to him or her that their conduct damages the network's interests.*

Many networks operate a Marketing Committee or similar body in addition to the FRC. The Marketing Committee is the forum where marketing strategies are mapped out jointly by the franchisor and elected franchisee representatives. Once again, decisions taken within such a forum stand a better chance of being accepted throughout the network than a 'directive' issued by the franchisor.

The franchisee lifecycle concept

This heading describes a phenomenon that has been well known in franchise circles for a very long time, yet nobody likes to talk about it. Essentially, the lifecycle concept tracks the development of the franchisor/franchisee relationship from its early beginnings to maturity. Various experts have labelled the various stages differently, but I don't think that it matters one iota. What I consider important is the fact that broadly speaking, they all come to the same conclusion: For the relationship to reach maturity, the franchisee needs to experience the full gamut of emotions I will describe below. A mature approach from both sides can help to shorten the process, but it seems to me that suppressing it would be unwise.

Insight

There seems to be consensus that by ignoring the franchisee lifecycle concept, it will go away. Having observed the franchise scene for more than three decades, I don't believe that this will ever happen. I decided, therefore, to shed some light on the topic in the hope that knowledge empowers.

INTRODUCING THE FRANCHISE E-FACTOR

Australian corporate psychologist and expert in franchise relations Greg Nathan did an in-depth study of the franchisor/franchisee relationship. He identified six distinct stages that take the relationship from initial dependence through a phase of independence to the blissful state of interdependence – franchising's equivalent to 7th heaven. He summarizes this as the E-factor and the figure below illustrates how it works.

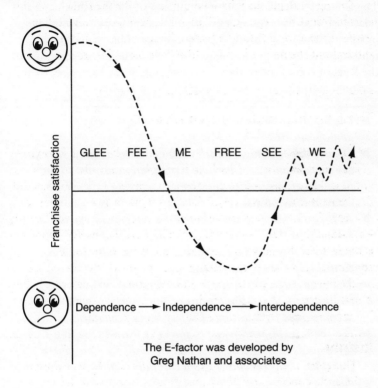

The E-factor was developed by
Greg Nathan and associates

The six stages in the franchise 'E-factor'

Greg Nathan, an internationally renowned franchise
adviser, psychologist and founder of the Franchise
Relationship Institute, has defined six stages of the
franchise relationships in a model he calls the franchise
E-factor. These are described in two of his books, *Profitable
Partnerships* and *The Franchise E-Factor*.

Greg Nathan writes:

The E-factor reflects the natural maturing of the franchise relationship as franchisees gain greater competence and confidence in running their franchises. It has six distinct phases and people tend to move through these stages at their own pace depending on the level of commitment they have to being in the franchise, their personal maturity and their communication skills.

- ▶ *During the* **Glee** *stage the franchisee will be nervous, excited and optimistic.*
- ▶ *During the* **Fee** *stage, which usually occurs about a year down the track, franchisees become particularly sensitive to the payment of fees, which they see as annoying expenses that eat away at their profits.*
- ▶ *As the franchisee moves into the* **Me** *stage he or she will typically be thinking that their success is due purely to their own hard work and effort and will tend to play down the contribution of the franchisor.*
- ▶ *The* **Free** *stage is characterized by a need to break free of the restrictions and limitations of the franchise and is usually accompanied by a testing of the system's boundaries.*
- ▶ *For the franchisee to move to the next, namely the* **See** *stage, there needs to be some frank and open discussions where franchisee and franchisor listen carefully to the other's point of view.*
- ▶ *From the* **See** *stage there is a natural progression to the* **We** *stage – a move from independent to interdependent thinking. At this point the franchisee recognizes that success and satisfaction generally come more easily from working with, rather than against, their franchisor.*

To reach the We stage a franchisee must be mature, objective, commercially minded and profitable. Franchisees who have negotiated their way through the franchise relationship minefield to the We stage are a franchise network's greatest asset.

Nathan then went on to develop a model that explains the frustrations franchisees feel – they are independent up to a point yet can't quite do as they please. The real value of Nathan's work lies in the fact that it helps franchisors and franchisees anticipate the inevitable and manage it to mutual benefit.

(More information about Greg Nathan's work and the franchise E-factor model can be found at www.franchiserelationships.com.)

THE TEN MOST IMPORTANT THINGS YOU NEED TO REMEMBER

1 *The franchise relationship is based on 'give and take' among equals. Neither the franchisor nor the franchisee can hope to achieve success in isolation.*

2 *Franchisees need to guard against losing sight of the fact that the proven success record of the franchisor had attracted them to the network in the first place. No matter how much you as a franchisee might think you know about the business, you cannot expect your franchisor to stand idly by if you start to tinker with the concept.*

3 *Successful franchisors can be relied upon to welcome input from franchisees. They will evaluate all ideas and implement those that have the potential to improve the competitiveness of the network as a whole. They will also acknowledge the franchisee's contribution.*

Insight

I was amazed to learn that most 'bestsellers' on the McDonald's menu were developed by the network's franchisees but always under the watchful eyes of head office staff.

4 *Western philosophy tends to emphasize the individual but in Islamic and other cultures, the family is seen as the basic building block of society. In the I Ching, the Chinese book of wisdom, it is said: 'When the family is in order, all the social relationships of mankind will be in order.' Wise words indeed and highly relevant to your situation as a franchisee because by joining a franchise, you are effectively joining a large family whose members look out for each other.*

5   *Remember that your franchisor is not a mind reader. If you need help, or something bothers you, say so.*

6   *You have every right to expect your franchisor to look out for your interests, but remember: Loyalty is a two-way street. If you come across a deal, or some information that does not concern you directly but would be of interest to the franchisor, pass the information on.*

7   *The members of a franchised network could do worse than to live by the credo coined by the three musketeers: All for one and one for all. Unless this happens, network cohesion will be in doubt and the brand will never reach its full potential.*

8   *Do not speak ill of the franchisor, fellow franchisees or the brand in public. If you have a problem with the brand, or an individual in the network's structure, sort it out in a face-to-face discussion. And whatever you do, remember that it is not a good idea to involve outsiders in family quarrels. On the other hand, if you cannot resolve a difference of opinion, ask a senior person, for example a veteran franchisee who enjoys the respect of both sides, to mediate.*

9   *Be willing to change. For franchised networks to prosper, they must keep at the forefront of change. You knew that when you joined and have no right to complain that, as a member of the family, you are expected to conform.*

10   *Take part in the activities of the Franchisee Representative Council or similar structure your network may operate in a pro-active and responsible manner. Your colleagues represent your interests so the least you can do is to attend the meetings they arrange. And if you do, you should not use your right to speak merely to vent petty issues. Focus on the bigger picture and make constructive suggestions on how the interests of the entire network could be served better.*

7

Where to turn for help

In this chapter you will learn:
- *whom to contact for assistance*
- *where to find up-to-date information on franchise opportunities*

Given franchising's success record and popularity, it is indeed surprising that the concept continues to be widely misunderstood. This is true not only in the UK but applies to most if not all countries around the world. I am reluctant to apportion blame for this unsatisfactory state of affairs but cannot shake off the feeling that erratic reporting in the media has something to do with it. This is certainly the opinion of an academic who conducted research into franchising and what people think about it. According to her, anecdotal evidence suggests that some franchisees are quite embarrassed to disclose their status. 'People don't know what a franchise is and if I tell them that I am part of a franchise network, they look at me funny,' one respondent observed.

Sources of information in the UK

Having worked through this book places you miles ahead of the pack, but don't stop here. The more you know about franchising the better equipped you will be to make an informed decision. You can turn to a large number of sources for information, and this chapter provides contact details of some. As you explore some of the websites I list, you are likely to experience the snowball effect – each site refers you to one or more additional sources.
The following suggestions will set you off on the right track.

▶ Most countries have a national franchise association; if there is one in your country then this should be your first port of call. Franchise associations offer information on their websites as well as in the form of print publications and videos. They also arrange seminars on franchising.

▶ Government-sponsored small business agencies provide information on franchising. In the UK, this is handled by the Department for Business Innovation (BIS); in other countries, the Department of Trade and Industry or similar agency fulfils this function.

▶ Franchise exhibitions are an excellent source of information. Your national franchise association will be able to tell you when the next such exhibition takes place in your area. When you visit such an exhibition, allow a full day; it will be worth it. There is a good chance that in addition to meeting franchisors face to face, you will be able to attend workshops on franchise-related topics and talk to professional advisors.

▶ In the UK and in most other countries, selected banks offer information on franchising. Franchise-friendly banks are an excellent source to tap into because they will be familiar with the local franchise scene and its main players. If they like a concept, they will offer you finance. If they don't, and assuming that your credit record is beyond reproach, you can safely conclude that there might be a problem with the franchisor.

▶ A good number of excellent websites deal with franchising.
  ▷ If you are a prospective franchisee looking for a franchise opportunity, you can access several websites that offer listings under various search criteria, for example industry sector, geographic location, investment level and so on.
  ▷ If you are a prospective franchisor and consider franchising as an expansion mechanism for your business, you will benefit from tapping into the same sites, firstly, to see what others in your field are up to, secondly, to obtain an insider's view of the franchise scene around the world.

CONTACT POINTS

The organizations listed below, arranged by country and then alphabetically, offer information on franchising. Some of them also deal with general small business issues. It is my understanding that an initial approach will not attract a fee but I would advise you to confirm this upfront.

Franchise information

- *The British Franchise Association (BFA)*
  Telephone 01865 379 892
  www.thebfa.org.uk
- *Business Support (Wales)*
  Telephone 0845 796 9798
  www.business-support-wales.gov.uk
- *Business Link (England)*
  Telephone 0845 600 9006
  www.businesslink.gov.uk
- *Business Gateway*
  Telephone 0845 609 6611
  www.bgateway.com
  whichfranchise.com
- *Information on franchising and franchise opportunities offered in a growing number of countries throughout the world*
  - ▷ *www.whichfranchise.com*
  - ▷ *www.whichfranchise.org*
  - ▷ *www.whichfranchise.ie*
  - ▷ *www.whichfranchise.co.za*
  - ▷ *www.ac-franchise.com*
  - ▷ *www.whichfranchise.net.au*

Government-assisted lending schemes

It happens frequently that an entrepreneur has a viable business plan but when he or she approaches a bank for finance, the bank rejects the application not because the applicant is unable to offer adequate surety.

To assist entrepreneurs that find themselves in this situation, governments in many countries make loan guarantees available that are usually accessible through participating banks. The precise rules for such lending schemes vary not only from one country to the next but also change over times. The following paragraphs provide an example of a loan guarantee offered by the UK government. It is best to discuss your actual needs with your bank as they will be familiar with the current rules in your country.

Enterprise Finance Guarantee

In the UK, the government currently offers the Enterprise Finance Guarantee as explained on page 82. Essentially it is an expanded version of the original Enterprise Finance Guarantee Scheme which has been terminated and the Small Firms Loan Guarantee Scheme which has been suspended.

Under the Enterprise Finance Guarantee scheme, the government guarantees 75 per cent of any loan granted by a participating bank to a qualifying small business. Franchisees of credible franchise networks have access to this scheme.

Applications must be made through a participating bank. The current list of lenders participating in the scheme at the time of going to print follows.

- ▶ *Airdrie Savings Bank*
- ▶ *Alliance and Leicester Commercial Bank*
- ▶ *Bank of Baroda*
- ▶ *Bank of Ireland (NI only)*
- ▶ *Bank of Scotland*
- ▶ *Barclays Bank*
- ▶ *Business Enterprise Fund*
- ▶ *Business Finance Solutions*
- ▶ *Clydesdale Bank*
- ▶ *The Co-operative Bank*
- ▶ *DSL Business Finance*

- GLE oneLondon
- HSBC
- Lloyds TSB
- NatWest
- NEL Fund Managers
- Northern Bank (NI only)
- The Royal Bank of Scotland
- State Securities
- South West Investment Group
- Triodos Bank
- UK Steel Enterprises
- Ulster Bank (NI Only)
- Venture Finance
- Whiteaway Laidlaw Bank
- Yorkshire Bank

The scheme will become available to other lenders as they apply. Delivery of the Enterprise Finance Guarantee, including the decision on whether or not it is appropriate to use it in connection with any specific lending transaction, is fully delegated to the participating lenders. There is no automatic entitlement to receive a guaranteed loan and nor is there any pre-qualification process for it.

OTHER FINANCE-RELATED CONTACTS

- *The website www.smallbusinesssuccess.biz offers a host of useful information, including ebooks on how to access small business grants, write a killer business plan and other business-related topics.*
- *The website www.bestmatch.co.uk puts you in touch with Business Angels, financiers who offer funding ranging from £10 000 to £250 000 in exchange for a share in the business and hands-on involvement in its running.*

International sources of franchise information

▶ **Deutscher Franchise Verband:** *Germany's national franchise association ranks among Europe's oldest. It oversees the orderly development of franchising in Germany and operates www.dfv-franchise.de. This site provides useful insights into franchising in Germany.*

▶ **European Franchise Federation (EFF):** *This is the federation of national franchise associations established in Europe. The website address is: www.eff.franchise.com.*

▶ **Franchise Association of South Africa:** *Established since 1979, this is South Africa's national franchise association. It plays a leading role in the orderly development of franchising throughout the African continent and can be contacted by visiting www.fasa.co.za.*

▶ **Franchise Direct:** *Ranks among the world's largest franchise portals – www.franchisedirect.com. The same organization also compiles the annual Franchise Europe Top 500 – visit www.franchiseeurope.com for further information.*

▶ **Franchising and Licensing Association (Singapore):** *Offers information on franchise issues of local interest. Visit www.flasingapore.org.*

▶ **International Franchise Association:** *Operates the website www.franchise.org. This site contains a host of information on franchising and although its focus is on franchising in the USA, it also contains contact details of national franchise associations active in countries around the globe.*

▶ **World Franchise Council:** *Has as its objective the enhancement of franchising globally. For more information visit www.worldfranchisecouncil.org.*

SOME MORE FRANCHISE-SPECIFIC WEBSITES

▶ *www.franchise-chat.com*
▶ *www.franchise-group.com*
▶ *www.franchise.org*
▶ *www.startup.wsj.com*
▶ *www.whichfranchise.com and sister sites*

Conclusion

Regardless of whether you want to become a franchisor or a franchisee, to enter the world of franchising has much merit. To achieve expected outcomes, however, you need to cut through the hype that is created by self-styled franchisors (if you are a prospective franchisee) and franchise consultants (if you are a prospective franchisor). The fact is that not every franchise constitutes a viable blueprint for business success, and not every business can be franchised.

As long as you enter franchising after a careful evaluation of all the facts at your disposal, it has the potential to become your first-class ticket to professional fulfilment and financial independence. The only thing left for me to say at this point is to wish you luck in your quest for entrepreneurship with a safety net. And remember: should you require clarification regarding the concept of franchising, not questions regarding a specific brand or franchise opportunity, you are welcome to email me: franchise@intekom.co.za.

Appendix 1 Preparing a business plan

Regardless of whether you become a franchisee or decide to go it alone, you know by now that when you approach a bank for finance, it will expect you to present a business plan. You might be reluctant to tackle this project because you heard someone say that it is a complex task. If so, I can only advise you not to believe everything you hear. Of course, business plans can be highly complex, and indeed some are, but this is overkill. Your business plan should be written simply and concisely to reflect your plans for the business. Drafting it will be well within your capabilities.

Tip

Your business plan should be a written outline of what you intend doing, what motivates you to do it, how you propose to implement your plan and what the financial implications of your project will be. You also need to deal with your product, its target market and why you think that people will buy from you rather than from your competition. Finally, your business plan needs to reflect your qualifications as well as those of your key people and your track records. This will go a long way towards convincing potential backers that you have what it takes to manage the project successfully.

Look hard enough and you will find an army of people out there who will offer to help you draw up your business plan. Your prospective franchisor will probably be among them. I advise you to turn them down, politely but firmly, because I believe that you are the best person to tackle this task. Of course, you should take input from your franchisor, your accountant and other advisors into account. When it comes to drafting the plan, however, it needs to reflect *your* capabilities and *your* dreams!

Contrary to what you might have been led to believe, your business plan is far more than a document that you are forced to draw up, rather grudgingly, because your bank manager asked for it. It is like a road map you can follow from point A, this being the beginning of your business venture, to the ultimate destination, a profitable business.

As your business grows, your plan will help you to stay on the right course by alerting you if actual performance in any one segment should deviate from the original plan. To enable you to stay on top of developments at all times, your business plan needs to be a living document you can use to monitor progress. It follows that your business plan needs to be frequently updated to reflect current realities.

Writing the business plan

> 'When you have collected all the facts and fears and you have made your decision, turn off your fears and go ahead!'
>
> General George Patton (1885–1945), US military leader

The 'go-ahead' part is obviously the exciting phase of becoming a franchisee but in the world of business, it is the nuts and bolts – in other words the boring stuff – that prevent the wheels from falling off. Take the business plan, for example. It is an indispensable requirement for operating a business, similar in its importance to the recipe for making that glorious dish. The chef is anxious to start cooking, but unless he or she has a detailed recipe, plus all the ingredients in correct proportions, the dish will not turn out as expected.

Layout considerations

Strictly speaking, there is no standard layout for a business plan, although most banks will require you to adhere to a specific format they have developed. This saves them time – they have become used to looking for certain information at a specific place. In the absence of a request from the banker, you cannot go wrong if you adhere to the layout suggested below. And even if the bank gives you a template, use it but work through this chapter anyway.

▶ *Doing so will enhance your overall understanding of what is required.*
▶ *It will also enable you to make your business plan stand out from others because you will know how to add some 'bells and whistles'.*

Knowing precisely where the business is at any given point in time, and where it is headed, financially and otherwise, will give you the confidence to make sound decisions. Moreover, your decisions will be based on facts rather than assumptions. The late American tennis great Arthur Ashe summed it up well when he said: 'One important key to success is self-confidence. An important key to self-confidence is careful preparation.'

Drafting the business plan

Even if you are in the fortunate position not to have to borrow money from the bank, you still need a business plan. Why? Because it will help you crystallize your thinking. In effect, you are embarking on a journey. If you don't decide early on where you want to go and plan your route carefully, how will you know when you have arrived? And how will you notice should you get lost along the way?

Keep the language simple and the layout business-like and you can't go wrong. And should a banker ask you to submit the plan using the bank's template, it will be a simple matter to transfer the information you already have into the banker's preferred format.

TITLE SHEET

State the name of your business and the date you compiled the plan. It is equally important to print your contact details either on the title sheet or on the first inside page of the document. This will help external readers of the plan to locate your contact details.

CONTENTS PAGE

On this page, list the headings of the various sections of the plan together with their respective page numbers.

THE BODY

This is the main part of the business plan. I have developed the following systematic approach to the creation of a business plan that will become your map to business success.

Executive summary
Use it to summarize the salient points of the project, with particular emphasis on the franchise arrangement. Bankers and other stakholders you will wish to interest in your project are busy people. More likely than not, they will read the executive summary first; should it fail to hold their interest, they might just move on to another project. It is in your interest to make this opening section exciting reading. However, you should do so without gushing and without straying from verifiable facts.

Clarify your business objectives
Set your business objectives out in a concise and achievable manner and stay clear of 'pie in the sky' scenarios. Business objectives are about facts, not fiction! Stick to what is attainable and likely to add up to 'money in the bank and sense' in the minds of your bank manager and other stakeholders.

Define your business concept

Before you go into detail, you should first be clear in your own mind what you plan to do and then provide readers of your business plan with an in-depth picture of your franchise and its potential.

▶ *Who is your franchisor and how well known is the network's brand?*

▶ *Is it a product-based business? Will you be setting up a processing section, for example a kitchen? Will you need a warehouse to store incoming goods, keep finished stock, and carry out packaging? Will you need to set up a distribution system and hire a sales force?*

▶ *Is it a service-based business? How will the service be marketed and delivered?*

▶ *What is the competitive edge of the business? What makes the franchise's product offering stand out from that of the competition?*

▶ *Do you need to purchase a product and if so, what are the supply arrangements? Is your franchisor the preferred supplier?*

▶ *Distribution: how you get your product to the end customer can make or break your new venture. The key is speed, efficiency and convenience – the customer's, not yours! Customers make no secret of the fact that they will support any company that gets things to them faster, more efficiently and conveniently. More often than not, price tends to be less important in customers' minds than reliable delivery, so make that your number one priority and explain in your plan how your network goes about this.*

▶ *How will you provide backup and handle warranty obligations? Where do the supplier's responsibilities end and yours begin?*

Explain the need to build after-sales relationships

The well-known adage that one happy customer will, at best, tell one or two other people about your excellent product and the sterling service they received, but will tell up to ten people if you offer poor service underlines the importance of after-sales service. How does your network handle this?

Refer to the protection of intellectual property

Many cases are on record of individuals who invented new products or designed a unique corporate identity for their business but omitted to protect their intellectual property. Unscrupulous people benefited from their hard work. As a franchisee, you need not worry about this; your franchisor will have taken care of it. By explaining this, and providing details of trademark registrations, for example, you show that you are aware.

Explain how brand identity is built

An important part of your business plan is a description of what makes the product or service unique. Describe the differentiating factors between your network's and its competitors' products. You should also explain that franchisors establish brands and replicate them quickly through the business format franchise model. This enables them to achieve rapid penetration of the target market and you plan to come along for the ride.

Provide an overview of your target market

Do you know where your market is and, more importantly, who your network's customers are? If so, say so – in great detail. Inexperienced business owners tend to generalize. They give the impression that they see their customers as faceless numbers that can be relied upon to purchase the product just so that they become rich. Unless you have a clear idea of who your network's customers are, it is like driving your motorcar in heavy fog, at high speed with your fog lights off. You will be driving blind, with an excellent chance of crashing the car in the process.

The mere fact that your sector might fall into the business-to-business market changes nothing. You need to appreciate the fact that even if the customer is a company, you will still be dealing with individuals. Just think about this for a moment: Have you ever seen a 'company' walk into a store and buy something? Of course not, and neither have I.

With the help of your franchisor, pose the following questions and formulate realistic answers to each one of them.

- ▶ Is there a market for your product in your territory? Be specific – is there really a gap in the market or are you just joining the fray for existing customers?
- ▶ Narrow down your target market. You might plan to sell to every person within your target market, and perhaps even those who drive past on their way to work, but this is unlikely to happen. In today's highly competitive markets, specialization is the name of the game. Focus on a clearly identified niche market.
- ▶ Does your market display potential for sustainable growth? If so, explain the reasons for your assertion. Changes in consumer lifestyles are often a good indicator of market trends. With everyone being perpetually on the go, products or services that save the consumer time and/ or add convenience are likely to be successful.
- ▶ How will you keep abreast of market trends? As it happens, your franchisor will do most of that, but you need to describe this in your business plan.
- ▶ If your business depends on site characteristics, say so and explain how you selected the proposed location. Many countries offer a wide range of climates and cultures. How did your franchisor make sure that the network's range appeals in your territory?
- ▶ Is the business affected by changing seasons? If so, does the network have a strategy in place to balance this out?
- ▶ Show awareness of your competition. Competition is healthy and I am not suggesting that you should fear your competition but you need to be aware of their activities and treat them with respect. Demonstrate in your business plan that you know that.

Define the infrastructure your business requires

Establish precisely what you will need to operate your business at peak efficiency, both in the short term and in the medium to longer term. It is best to build expansion capacity into your plan or you might encounter bottlenecks. When you describe how your business will operate, make mention of the procedures manual your franchisor will supply.

Explain the marketing plan

Describe how your franchisor markets the brand, and how you plan to tap into the franchisor's activities to maximize customer response in your territory.

Financial issues

After planning and dreaming to your heart's content, you are now ready to convert your plans into financial reality.

- ▶ *Prepare a financial forecast:*
  - ▷ *Project profit/loss and cash flow for year one in detail. Be sure to explain assumptions you have made, for example, level of sales, payment terms granted to your customers, payment terms granted to you by your suppliers and other working capital needs.*
  - ▷ *How soon do you expect to reach break-even? (Break-even means that 'cash inflows' and 'cash outflows' are equal – the business creates neither a profit nor a loss.)*
  - ▷ *Project profit/loss for years 2 and 3 in approximate figures.*
- ▶ *Comment on the issue of cash flow. Will you have enough capital to start your business and keep it operational until the cash flow is strong enough to sustain it? If not, how much do you need to borrow and how do you propose to go about this?*

At this point, I must stress that the preparation of detailed financial projections is crucial to the success of your venture. Not only will your banker scrutinize them when he or she assesses your loan proposal but you also need them to keep score on an ongoing basis.

What makes you tick?

I mentioned earlier that no matter whether you are dealing with end-users or companies, you always deal with people. Indeed, every type of business is built on relationships, and banking is no exception. Your bankers will naturally want to know that your project is viable and that your finances are realistic, but there is more.

Progressive bankers will want to know who you are and what makes you really tick. Portray yourself as the passionate human being you are, assure them that you strive for excellence in every respect and your success chances will multiply.

Your support network

Under this heading, you will refer to your franchisor and explain the support infrastructure you will be entitled to draw on. Next, list business partners, members of your key staff and professional advisers and their qualifications. You could also describe the nature of the various relationships, and why these individuals can be relied upon to support you.

APPENDIX

The appendix should contain detailed schedules of financial projections, market research data, sales projections and other supporting documentation that serves to support your assumptions. You might also want to include copies of your vision and your mission statement for the business, and your personal CV.

Avoid the following pitfalls

Business plans are nothing new. Bankers have seen hundreds if not thousands of them and tell me that they range in quality from compelling to pathetic. I cannot see any valid reason why new entrepreneurs should not learn from the mistakes their predecessors have made, so I asked some bankers to list their pet hates when it comes to business plans. Their feedback strongly suggests that you should avoid the following:

▶ *Drafting a plan that is strong on buzzwords but lacks facts and soul.*
▶ *Showing reluctance to take ownership of the plan by failing to accept responsibility for the delivery of the proposed outcomes.*

- ▶ Focusing on details of the plan long before a general direction has been set.
- ▶ Omitting details, often in a transparent attempt to fudge issues that could be construed as negative rather than dealing with them head-on.
- ▶ Proposing solutions without defining measurable outcomes.
- ▶ Failing to commit to realistic target dates and divide into traceable progress steps.
- ▶ Taking things for granted by omitting to list steps that will clearly be necessary.
- ▶ Using industry jargon, thereby making the arrogant assumption that unless the reader is an expert in this particular sector, he or she must be stupid.
- ▶ Including facets of the business that are either irrelevant, or are entered with no real intention of pursuing them further.
- ▶ Permitting the writer's prejudices to affect suggested outcomes.
- ▶ Stating facts that are patently incorrect, in an attempt to promote a certain course of action.
- ▶ Omitting to record negative facts. It is generally better to acknowledge their presence and propose realistic measures designed to counteract them.
- ▶ Inviting comment by posing questions when the desired outcome appears to be a foregone conclusion.
- ▶ Sloppy presentation, facts that do not tally, poor spelling and grammar.

It is not difficult to avoid these traps. By doing so, you give yourself a head start in the race to win your potential financial backer's support.

Appendix 2 Recommended best practices

Although every effort has been made to ensure that this guide conforms to the requirements of codes of conduct published by various national franchise associations, it is not binding upon anyone and does not purport to be an officially sanctioned publication. Rather, it is based on work I undertook at the behest of an agency of the South African Department of Trade and Industry (DTI). As a service to readers, I have modified it to meet international expectations. The original document can be accessed on www.seda.co.za.

Franchisor

1 PRELIMINARY STAGE

Before considering franchising as an option for business expansion, the prospective franchisor should be able to provide positive answers to the following statements:

1.1 *The business has been operating profitably for at least one year and compelling evidence exists that it is ready for expansion.*
1.2 *Operational aspects pertaining to the production, handling and delivery of the product or service as well as the business management systems required to control operations have been optimized.*

1.3 *Business processes have been standardized and simplified to such an extent that it is possible to train an inexperienced person in their use within a reasonably short period.*

1.4 *A brand has been created and registered that is either well established already or shows realistic potential for rapid development.*

1.5 *A well-defined market for the product or service exists and there are clear indications that the demand curve is on a sustainable upward trend.*

1.6 *The target market population for the product or service is of adequate size and the market is structured in such a way that the establishment of a reasonable number of delivery points in quick succession appears to be commercially viable.*

1.7 *The product or service possesses some aspect of uniqueness that makes it difficult for copycat operators to flood the market with imitation products.*

1.8 *Profit margins within the industry sector are sufficiently robust to enable the prospective franchisor as well as his/her future franchisees to earn attractive returns.*

1.9 *The prospective franchisor is prepared to make a sizeable investment in the establishment of the franchise infrastructure and is willing to take a long-term view regarding expected returns.*

1.10 *The prospective franchisor recognizes that every network's success depends on the creation of win–win outcomes for franchisor and franchisees. In operating the franchise, the prospective franchisor undertakes to espouse the principles expressed in relevant national franchise association's Code of Ethics and Business Practices or similar document.*

1.11 *Before the franchise will be launched, the prospective franchisor will operate at least one pilot outlet, this being a company-owned outlet that will be operated at arm's length to test the viability of the operation.*

2 PREPARING THE FRANCHISE PACKAGE

Assuming that the above questions can be answered satisfactorily, work on the development of the franchise package can begin. This phase will include the following tasks:

2.1 *Establishing the network's potential*
The market potential of the franchise must be established in detail, culminating in the creation of a network expansion plan. This can be broken down further into:

    2.1.1 *Identifying target areas for expansion.*

    2.1.2 *Assessing the potential of each target area.*

    2.1.3 *Ranking areas by potential, giving due cognisance to possible logistical constraints which could impact negatively on the franchisor's ability to service and support franchisees in an area.*

    2.1.4 *Putting a timeline to the development plan, giving due consideration to commercial realities.*

    2.1.5 *Throughout this process, care will be taken to guard against the potential over-saturation of an area.*

2.2 *Testing the viability of the project*
The viability of the franchise will be tested by means of creating financial projections that reflect, firstly, anticipated performance levels attainable by the franchisor and, secondly, anticipated performance levels of future franchisees, as follows:

    2.2.1 *Drawing up projections of franchise development and operational costs versus projected income from franchising over the first three to five years of operations.*

    2.2.2 *Drawing up projections pertaining to the financial performance of a typical franchisee of the network, projected for at least three years into the future. Projections should incorporate a projected cashflow and income statement.*
    At this stage, projections will have to be based on the known performance of the franchisor's company-owned units and/or pilot outlets but will be adjusted to reflect the realities of the various target territories. (In keeping with acceptable forecasting practice, projections for the first year should be detailed, but will become increasingly vague as they extend further into the future.)

    2.2.3 *Should a separate company be formed to oversee the franchise roll-out process, the prospective franchisor will draw up a balance sheet that will reflect the capital structure of this company at the start-up stage.*

(Should no new company be formed, a recent balance sheet of the holding company must be available.)

2.3 *Setting of franchise fees*

Based on the calculations described in paragraph 2.2, initial and ongoing fees will be set, subject to the following considerations:

2.3.1 *The initial or upfront fee is a once-off fee, payable by the franchisee on signing of the contract.*

2.3.1.1 *The initial fee will be set as a fixed amount that will be the same for each applicant. It is acceptable, however, to increase the initial fee over time to reflect the growing awareness the brand enjoys.*

2.3.1.2 *The amount expressed in monetary terms will be set to allow the franchisor to recoup the cost of creating the franchise package on a pro-rata basis from early franchisees, with the calculations based on the projected number of outlets expected to come on stream during the first three to five years.*

2.3.2 *The management services fee must cover the costs arising from ongoing franchisee support and allow the franchisor to make a profit. (Experience suggests that the franchise operation will become profitable only once a certain number of franchises are operational, and the franchisor is aware of this.)*

2.3.2.1 *The management services fee is an ongoing fee, payable either weekly or monthly.*

2.3.2.2 *It will be set as a percentage of franchisees' sales.*

2.3.2.3 *To set the management services fee as a fixed fee expressed in monetary terms removes the element of joint risk-taking from the franchise relationship and is ordinarily not recommended.*

2.3.3 *Every network will operate a marketing fund or similar structure which is to be funded through equal contributions made by the network's franchisees and the franchisor's company-owned business units.*

2.3.3.1 *Contributions will either be set as a percentage of each unit's sales or as a fixed monthly payment expressed in monetary terms.*

2.3.3.2 *The fund will be administered by a marketing committee that will consist of franchisor and franchisee representatives; it is customary for the franchisor to retain the casting vote.*

2.3.3.3 *Subject to the network having an adequate number of franchisees, franchisee representatives will be elected by their peers.*

2.3.3.4 *Monies received by the fund will be used exclusively to pay for network-wide product advertising and other initiatives as decided upon by the marketing committee.*

2.4 *The compilation of the operations and procedures manual*
The operations and procedures manual (OPM) is the document that ensures operational consistency throughout the network.

2.4.1 *The OPM will contain a clear and detailed description of every operational step franchisees are expected to implement. Without limiting the scope of the OPM, this will include all aspects of product/service delivery as well as the operation and maintenance of the systems and procedures needed to administer and control the business and prepare required reports.*

2.4.2 *The OPM will be delivered to franchisees in a format that is conducive to quick and easy access. Presentation in hard copy format is recommended, but delivery in electronic format, either via the network's Intranet or by magnetic medium (CD or DVD) is acceptable. Ideally, hard copy format should be supplemented by electronic delivery.*

2.4.3 *It is the franchisor's responsibility to keep the OPM up to date to ensure that it always reflects current practices.*

2.5 *The franchise agreement*
In recognition of slight variations in the legal treatment of franchise arrangements, comment pertaining to the franchise

agreement has been omitted. However, guidelines should be available from your national franchise association.

2.6 *The disclosure document*

> **Insight**
>
> **Author note:** In the UK, the creation of a formal disclosure document is not a binding requirement. However, a growing number of enlightened franchisors provide one.

Dealings between franchisor and franchisees must be open and honest throughout, and it is recognized that a disclosure document is an important written expression of this fundamental principle. For this reason, it is recommended that every franchisor should strive to issue prospective franchisees with a disclosure document that contains at least the following information.

> **2.6.1** *An introduction to the franchisor's organization:*
>> **2.6.1.1** *A full description of the nature of the company's business, the company's registered name, postal and street address, a history of the business including the year it was founded and details of companies that are affiliated to it.*
>> **2.6.1.2** *The names, addresses and qualifications of the company's shareholders and directors, their respective business experience and track record, especially but not only as it pertains to operating a franchise.*
>> **2.6.1.3** *Details of trademarks, patents and other relevant intellectual property the company owns and wishes to introduce into the franchise package.*
>> **2.6.1.4** *A certificate signed by the company's auditors that testifies to the financial stability of the company. Furthermore, a statement to be placed into the body of the disclosure document and signed by a director/member of the company will refer to this certificate*

and warrant that the financial position of the company has not materially changed since the date the auditor's certificate was issued.

2.6.1.5 Should the franchisor be a member of the national franchise association, membership details will be given. If the franchisor is not a member of the local franchise association, a brief statement setting out the reasons should be included.

2.6.1.6 Details of any other professional organizations, if any, the franchisor is a member of.

2.6.2 A schedule of the investment a prospective franchisee is expected to make, broken down as follows:

2.6.2.1 Initial fee. If the initial fee is a fixed fee, the amount payable in monetary terms. Should the initial fee be variable (not recommended – please refer to paragraph 2.3.1), the basis for the calculation of the fee will be explained. Payment terms and conditions under which the initial fee might become refundable, be it in full or in part, should this possibility be contemplated, will be provided.

2.6.2.2 Set-up cost. This is the total amount of funds required to set up the business. It will be further broken down into the cost of land or buildings, equipment, furnishings, fittings and initial stock, as applicable. Should the franchisor intend to control disbursements, be it in full or in part, this must be clearly stated and an explanation given of how this will be administered.

2.6.2.3 Training fees. Should the cost of initial training not be included in the initial fee but be charged out as a separate amount, the amount payable for the training of the franchisee and/or the franchisee's staff must be shown.

2.6.2.4 *Working capital. Under this heading, the amount of working capital the prospective franchisee is expected to provide will be stated, expressed in monetary terms.*

2.6.2.5 *Follow-up investments. Under this heading, an indication will be given of how soon after commencing business the franchisee will be forced to make further investments into the business unit's infrastructure and/or provide additional working capital.*

2.6.2.6 *Franchisee's minimum contribution. With reference to the total capital requirement, franchisor will state:*
  ▷ *The percentage of the total investment the franchisee is expected to make available in unencumbered cash.*
  ▷ *The type of financing options offered by the franchisor, if any, and the terms and conditions attached thereto.*
  ▷ *What other assistance, for example by way of an introduction to a banker, or in the form of giving hands-on help with the drafting of the business plan, the franchisor offers.*

2.6.3 *Ongoing fees*

2.6.3.1 *The level of management services fee payable, the basis for the computation of this fee and the payment terms.*

2.6.3.2 *Contributions to the advertising fund, broken down as follows:*
  ▷ *Fee level and on what basis contributions will be computed.*
  ▷ *How the advertising fund will be administered.*
  ▷ *A statement setting out whether the franchisee will be obliged to spend additional monies on local advertising. If so, the minimum amount, either in*

monetary terms or as a percentage of sales, to be spent over a specified period, must be stated.

2.6.3.3 A statement by the franchisor to the effect that no other fees will be levied unless it is agreed upon between the franchisor and the majority of the franchisees in the network at that time that:

▷ Franchisees receive a genuine benefit;

▷ The payment does not erode franchisee's profitability;

▷ The additional fee does not constitute a case of 'double-dipping' in the hands of the franchisor.

2.6.3.4 The question of renewal fees (that is a fee to be levied should the franchisee make use of an option to renew the franchise agreement beyond the initial period) is currently a hotly debated issue. To charge renewal fees is relatively common in some countries, less so in others. Consider the following:

▷ The creation of win–win outcomes is a credo of franchising.

▷ Proponents of renewal fees claim that if a franchisee wishes to renew the agreement on expiry, it indicates that the franchise is profitable. The franchisor builds the brand and should therefore be entitled to compensation for making it available for a further period.

▷ The compelling counter-argument is that if franchisors want to share, directly or indirectly, in franchisees' profits, they should be prepared to share their potential losses as well.

▷ Consensus exists that should a renewal fee be levied, full details must be given in the disclosure document.

2.6.4 *Financial projections*
Financial projections that are contained in the disclosure document and purport to illustrate the expected business performance of the franchise must give detailed answers to the following questions:

2.6.4.1 *Are the figures given, especially with respect to projected sales, based on the franchisor's experience in general, or do they constitute actual performance figures of a specific business unit?*

2.6.4.2 *What is the relevance of the figures given in relation to the expected potential of the territory under negotiation?*

2.6.4.3 *Do the projections include some or all of the following: franchisee's drawings, depreciation charges, interest on loans, capital repayments?*

2.6.4.4 *Has the impact of taxation been taken into account? If not, this must be stated.*

2.6.4.5 *This portion of the disclosure document will also contain the following statement: 'The figures given are projections only, with the actual business results the franchisee can expect to achieve being dependent on the franchisee's ability and hard work. The franchisor does not warrant that the territory under negotiation will produce similar figures to those shown in the projections.'*

2.6.5 *References the franchisee and/or his/her professional advisers can follow up on, including:*

2.6.5.1 *The name of the franchisor's bankers, complete with contact details.*

2.6.5.2 *A list of the network's established franchisees and their contact details.*

2.6.5.3 *A list of franchisees that have left the network during the past two years, complete with contact details. Should current contact details of some ex-franchisees not be* available, a written statement setting out the circumstances under which the franchise was terminated must be given and will be deemed to form part of the disclosure document.

2.6.5.4 A statement to the effect that the prospective franchisee is authorized to approach any one or all of the referees the franchisor has provided and make enquiries regarding the commercial soundness of the franchisor company and the viability of the network's business, with specific reference to the territory under negotiation.

2.6.6 The disclosure document will contain a comprehensive description of the initial and ongoing assistance the franchisor intends to offer, for example:

2.6.6.1 Details of initial training including training of franchisee's staff if applicable and information on the accreditation status of such training.

2.6.6.2 The extent of assistance pertaining to site selection and lease negotiations.

2.6.6.3 The extent of assistance with the drafting of specifications for the fitting-out and equipping of the business unit.

2.6.6.4 Details of ongoing training including training of franchisee's staff, including the following information:
   ▷ Is participation compulsory or voluntary?
   ▷ Where will the training take place?
   ▷ Is the franchisee expected to contribute towards costs of training? If so, how will such costs be determined?
   ▷ What is the accreditation status of the training offered?

2.6.6.5 Comprehensive details of planned and ad hoc site visits, regional and national meetings.

2.6.6.6 Schedule of network-specific reporting requirements, their extent and frequency.

2.6.6.7 *Details of proposed joint purchasing arrangements, marketing drives and other network-wide activities, together with a statement setting out:*
  ▷ *Whether participation is compulsory or voluntary.*
  ▷ *Whether the franchisor receives any benefits from making these arrangements.*
  ▷ *What recourse franchisees have, should products supplied by the franchisor or suppliers nominated by the franchisor be overpriced.*
  (An acceptable safeguard would be a clause along the lines suggested in paragraph 3.2.6.2.)

2.6.7 *A copy of the franchise agreement must be attached to the disclosure document.*

2.6.8 *Together with the disclosure document, the prospective franchisee will receive a recognized information brochure that explains how franchising works, and a copy of the relevant national franchise association's Code of Ethics and Business Practices or equivalent.*

2.6.9 *The disclosure document will be dated and signed by an authorized officer of the franchisor company.*

2.6.10 *The disclosure document will be updated annually, or 30 days after material changes in the situation of the franchisor company have occurred, whichever comes first.*

2.7 *Setting up the franchise*

Prospective franchisors recognize that an adequately resourced franchisee support function is central to the success of the network. The overall capacity of the franchisee support function should always be kept one step ahead of actual requirements. The following are minimum requirements:

2.7.1 *Infrastructure*
  The required number of support staff will be governed by the nature of the industry sector and the number of franchisees to be supported; the overriding

requirement is that franchisees receive the level of support they are entitled to.

The franchisee support office should offer adequate facilities for the conduct of meetings and training sessions.

2.7.2 *Company-owned business unit*

It is essential that the franchisor enjoys unfettered access to at least one business unit to ensure that:

2.7.2.1 *Face-to-face contact with end-users is maintained.*

2.7.2.2 *New products, systems and procedures can be developed and tested before being released into the network of franchisees.*

2.7.2.3 *Prospective franchisees can be offered an opportunity to work at a business unit for a few days; this will enable them to obtain first-hand experience of what life as an operator of this type of business would be like. At the same time, franchisor representatives can observe the prospect in action, thereby assessing his or her suitability.*

2.7.2.4 *New franchisees and their staff can be given hands-on operational training in an environment that is controlled by the franchisor. To use a unit owned by a franchisee for these purposes is less than ideal because franchisees have a business to run and should be left to get on with this task. A company-owned unit is ideal for this purpose. Alternatively, a joint venture with a franchisee would be acceptable.*

2.8 *Marketing the franchise*

Honesty, truth and trust are the foundations of franchising, and the network's approach to marketing the opportunity must reflect that

2.8.1 *Establishing the franchisee profile*

To ensure that the promotional message reaches the

correct target group, an ideal franchisee profile will be established first.

2.8.1.1 The profile will be based strictly on operational requirements.

2.8.1.2 Discrimination or prejudice in any manner or form will be avoided.

2.8.1.3 The profile will be applied across the board, with specific regard to programmes designed to assist members of minority groupings.

2.8.2 Promotional materials

All promotional materials will be designed keeping in mind how the target audience is likely to interpret the information they contain.

2.8.2.1 As a minimum requirement, literature, videos and other promotional materials will be presented in the official local language; in addition, the material may be offered in other official languages if appropriate.

2.8.2.2 Information will be factual and provide prospects with an accurate reflection of what to expect as a franchisee, warts and all.

2.8.2.3 Newspaper advertisements must conform to the relevant section of the Code of Advertising Practice published by the national Advertising Standards Authority or similar body if it exists.

2.8.2.4 Prospects will be informed at the earliest opportunity of the approximate investment level and what other resources they are expected to provide.

2.8.2.5 Should marketing materials contain performance figures then it will be clearly stated whether these figures are based on assumptions or reflect actual figures achieved by a specific unit. Should the latter apply, the location of the unit or the demographic profile of the area within which it is located will be stated.

2.8.3 *Franchise sales*
Franchisors recognize that it would not only be unethical but also detrimental to the long-term development of their networks, should unsuitable individuals be admitted as franchisees.

2.8.3.1 *Prospects will be carefully evaluated to ascertain, as far as possible, that they possess the required personality, professional background, experience and adequate resources to operate a business unit of the network with a reasonable chance of success.*

2.8.3.2 *Promising prospects will be:*
▷ *Provided with all the information they need to reach an informed decision.*
▷ *Encouraged to discuss the opportunity with their professional advisers.*
▷ *Encouraged to spend time at a business unit owned by the franchisor to facilitate realistic assessment by both parties.*

2.8.3.3 *Before being asked to make a final decision, promising prospects will be encouraged to spend time with existing franchisees of the network to learn first hand what life as a franchisee of the network will be like.*

2.8.3.4 *Under no circumstances will prospects be pressured into signing the franchise agreement without having evaluated all underlying factors first. A minimum of two weeks will be allowed to lapse between the date a prospect has received the network's disclosure document and franchise agreement and the date the prospect will be permitted to:*
▷ *Enter into any binding obligation (except for the signing of a confidentiality undertaking intended to protect the franchisor against industrial espionage).*
▷ *Sign the franchise agreement and/or make any payments.*

2.8.3.5   *Should the nature of the industry sector make the franchise site-dependent and no acceptable site is available at the time the prospect is ready to sign the franchise agreement, the prospect will be alerted to this fact. Should the prospect be willing to proceed regardless, he or she will be directed to pay the initial fee into a duly constituted trust account where it will be held until a site can be found.*

3 OPERATING THE FRANCHISE

The focus of the franchise operation can never be the mere shifting of a product or service, but the creation and maintenance of a tightly controlled and flawlessly executed system designed to enhance the business performance of franchisees. The following examples illustrate this:

3.1   *Initial assistance*
The franchisor recognizes that the franchisee is at his/her most vulnerable at this point and will provide generous assistance. The form this will take is industry-specific but will include some or all of the following:

    3.1.1   *Franchisee finance*
    The franchisor will work with prospective franchisees to prepare a business plan that is likely to meet the expectations of providers of finance, facilitate introductions to banks and assist with the subsequent negotiations.

    3.1.2   *Training*
    The franchisor recognizes that the better prepared the new franchisee is for the task ahead the better his/her success chances will be. To this end, the franchisor will:

        3.1.2.1   *Prepare a formal training course that covers all facets of successful operation.*
        3.1.2.2   *Arrange for the presentation of the course in accordance with a formal training schedule*

and in an environment that is conducive to learning.

3.1.2.3 Conduct frequent assessments to ensure that the new franchisee internalizes the training material.

3.1.2.4 Offer additional training to new franchisees who take longer than expected to absorb necessary skills. Such assistance should be supplied free of charge; it is acceptable, however, to compel the franchisee to carry his/her own costs arising from accommodation and meals.

3.1.3 Site selection
Should location be a critical success factor, the franchisor will use proven site selection techniques to secure optimal sites for franchisees. This will be followed by assistance in negotiating a lease at the most advantageous terms possible.

3.1.4 Equipping the new business unit
The franchisor will assist with the drafting of specifications and facilitate introduction to suitable vendors, bearing in mind that at this stage, the typical franchisee will lack experience and depends on the franchisor's advice.

3.1.5 Pre-opening procedures
The franchisor will work closely with the franchisee to:

3.1.5.1 Draw up proper specifications for the ordering, installation and commissioning of equipment, fixtures and fittings.

3.1.5.2 Assist with the ordering, receiving and merchandising of initial stock.

3.1.5.3 Help to recruit and train staff.

3.1.5.4 Ensure that all systems and procedures are in place.

3.1.5.5 Initiate an initial marketing drive and prepare the business for the grand opening.

3.1.5.6 Grand opening and beyond
On the day of the 'grand opening' and

throughout the days/weeks that follow, a franchisor representative will spend time at the franchisee's unit to ensure smooth operation of the business. As the franchisee's confidence increases, the frequency of these visits will decrease until the franchise can be integrated into the ongoing franchisee support schedule.

3.2 *Ongoing support*

The following are examples only – the nature and extent of actual franchisee support franchisors are expected to provide depends on the needs of the specific industry sector.

3.2.1 *Trouble-shooting*

To ensure that members of a franchised network receive assistance in dealing with operational problems, an experienced individual will be available throughout the network's standard business hours to offer guidance to franchisees who experience operational difficulties.

3.2.2 *Site visits*

3.2.2.1 *Representatives of the franchisor will make periodic scheduled visits to each franchisee's site to ascertain that everything functions as intended, and offer assistance where it does not.*

3.2.2.2 *Should reasonable suspicion, arising for example as a result of a complaint received from a dissatisfied customer, exist that the franchisee is lax in following prescribed procedure, unscheduled visits are in order. Such interventions should nevertheless focus on assisting the franchisee to meet accepted standards.*

3.2.3 *Maintaining channels of communication*

3.2.3.1 *The franchisor will facilitate ongoing and efficient communication between the support office and members of the network using* *electronic channels, telephone and fax communications and newsletters.*

3.2.3.2 *The franchisor will schedule regular regional meetings to exchange ideas on developments of regional interest, and facilitate cooperation among neighbouring franchisees.*

3.2.3.3 *At least once annually, the franchisor will arrange a national meeting of all franchisees to exchange ideas on developments within the network and discuss strategies for the year ahead.*

3.2.4 *Mentoring*
A senior member of the franchisor's team will meet with each franchisee periodically, but not less than twice a year, on an individual basis to review the franchises' business performance. Where appropriate, constructive criticism will be offered, followed by an earnest effort to map out a course of action designed to resolve an unsatisfactory situation.

3.2.5 *Intensive care*
Should a franchisee experience serious operational or financial problems, the franchisor will intervene speedily and with a view to salvaging the situation. The type of intervention will depend on individual circumstances, but could include:

3.2.5.1 *The drawing-up of a rescue plan which, for example, could be linked to the rescheduling of debt.*

3.2.5.2 *The granting of technical assistance, which could involve temporary secondment of senior operations staff.*

3.2.5.3 *Assistance with the sale of the unit; such an intervention should aim to minimize potential damage to the brand and/or keep financial losses suffered by the franchisee in check.*

3.2.5.4 *Should problems be recurring or widespread, franchisors should seek assistance from reputable franchise experts.*

3.2.6 *Group purchasing schemes*
In suitable circumstances, the franchisor will negotiate network-wide deals with key suppliers, for the benefit of all members of the network. Two important provisos apply:

> **3.2.6.1** *The franchisor will disclose upfront any benefits he/she stands to receive from entering into arrangements that compel franchisees to purchase goods or services from the franchisor or from vendors prescribed by the franchisor.*

> **3.2.6.2** *Should a franchisee be able to obtain goods or services of identical quality from a legitimate source that is sustainable and accessible to all members of the network, at a substantially lower price than the franchisor or a vendor charge, the franchisee will have the right to purchase from this source. Subject to realities prevalent in the industry sector, a price difference is defined as being substantial if it is equal to or in excess of 5 per cent of the customary gross profit margin usually achieved on the product or service.*

3.2.7 *Joint marketing*
Joint marketing and brand building efforts are an integral part of any franchise arrangement. Consequently, franchisors will:

> **3.2.7.1** *Monitor developments in the market place and make their findings conveniently accessible to all members of the network.*

> **3.2.7.2** *Industry sector realities permitting, develop new products and services designed to strengthen the network's standing in the market place.*

> **3.2.7.3** *Conduct suitable promotional and advertising drives, conceptualized and implemented in close cooperation with all*

members of the network or their authorized representatives, for example the FRC.

3.2.7.4 *Develop a range of promotional programmes that can be customized by franchisees for use in their local/regional promotional drives.*

3.3 *Network expansion*

This is one of the few areas in franchising where the interests of the franchisor and the franchisees do not necessarily mesh. While the network stands to benefit from an increase in the number of outlets because it increases overall sales, the individual franchisee's profitability could suffer if the gain in market share is less than the increase in costs the establishment and operation of an additional unit causes. Although network growth tends to translate into increased buying power and brand awareness and is therefore in the interest of all members of the network, the franchisor has a moral duty to protect individual franchisees against competition from within the network as far as possible. To offer a franchisee a first right of refusal to establish an additional outlet in close proximity to the one he or she already owns is an option but it is not always the answer. The following guidelines will help franchisors to deal with the resulting dilemma.

3.3.1 *The establishment of new franchised outlets in close proximity to established competitors could create problems and franchisors recognize that. If it is strategically necessary to locate a unit in a seemingly over-traded area, it should be operated as a company-owned unit first. Only once its viability has been proven should it be sold to a franchisee.*

3.3.2 *The establishment of additional business units, whether under franchise or company-owned, in close proximity to established units of the network, known as encroachment, must be avoided. This would lead to members of the same network competing for the same customers. Petty jealousies would surface and confusion would reign.*

3.3.3 *Franchisors should guard against locking franchisees into franchise expansion deals (an obligation to open a*

predetermined number of units within a specified time
frame) if it becomes obvious that this step exceeds the
franchisee's capabilities and resources.

3.3.4 *Should growth strategies create a conflict between the*
interests of an established franchisee and the need to
expand the network, the franchisor should make every
reasonable effort to adequately protect the franchisee's
legitimate interests, but without sacrificing the interests
of the network as a whole.

4 RELATIONSHIP MATTERS

4.1 *Relations between franchisor and franchisees will be*
conducted in an atmosphere of goodwill and cooperation,
with trust and open lines of communication playing an
important part.

4.1.1 *Franchisees' right to be heard*
Franchisees are entrepreneurs in their own right and
cannot be treated like salaried managers. Rather
than mapping out a course of action and imposing it
on them, the franchisor will debate issues of mutual
concern and strive to achieve consensus if possible.

4.1.2 *Franchisee representation*
The franchisor recognizes that network growth could
cause anxiety among some franchisees who might
feel alienated. The inevitable delegation of day-to-
day interaction between franchisor and individual
franchisees to members of the franchise support team
could add to this feeling of unease. To address this, the
franchisor will encourage the formation of a franchisee
representative committee (FRC) or similar structure
early on. This is a franchisor initiative with franchisee
representation that looks after the interests of the
network and its stakeholders.

4.2 *Conflict prevention/resolution*
The franchisor recognizes that the franchise relationship is an
intensely personal one, and that conflicts are bound to arise
from time to time. It is in the interest of all parties to resolve

such conflicts speedily and fairly while striving for a win–win outcome. The following guidelines apply:

4.2.1 *Advance warning*
Should a franchisee infringe against his/her obligations under the franchise agreement, he/she should be advised of this and, circumstances permitting, allowed a reasonable period to remedy the infringement.

4.2.2 *Should the franchisor be the offending party, the franchisor should appoint a director or senior manager to look into the complaint and endeavour to negotiate a solution that is acceptable to both parties.*

4.2.3 *Should the parties find it impossible to arrive at a mutually acceptable solution, or if an action of one party has caused a serious breakdown of trust, disputes shall be referred for mediation or arbitration.*

5 *THE FRANCHISOR'S OBLIGATION TO LEAD*

Franchisees join a network because they want to be part of a successful organization. This means that the franchisor has a moral obligation to strive for performance excellence and market leadership within the network. In addition, it is in the interest of franchisors to stay informed about developments in the franchise sector in general, to be prepared to actively participate in sector initiatives and generally conduct their businesses in a manner that is likely to foster franchising's reputation and continued growth.

Franchisees

When it comes to the implementation of best practices, franchisors cannot succeed in isolation. Not only have franchisees an important role to play, they have indeed an obligation to find out what to expect from a franchisor and what will be expected of them in return. The following paragraphs will shed some light on this.

1 FRANCHISEE'S EARLY OBLIGATIONS

Most of the disputes that arise between a franchisor and a franchisee are caused by a lack of understanding of the basic principles on which the franchise relationship is based. Adherence to the following guidelines should go a long way towards minimizing misunderstandings of this nature.

1.1 *Preparations*
    1.1.1 *Before investigating a specific franchise opportunity, prospective franchisees should ensure that they are familiar with the basic principles of franchising. Quality information is available from national franchise associations and several websites – see Chapter 7.*
    1.1.2 *Following an in-depth analysis of his/her resources, personal likes and dislikes, the prospective franchisee will be in a better position to decide whether to pursue the franchise route.*
    1.1.3 *Based on the insights gained from this self-assessment exercise, the prospective franchisee will decide which type of franchise he or she should investigate.*
1.2 *Assessing opportunities*
The prospective franchisee recognizes that for a franchise relationship to prosper, it must be based on mutual trust and respect. It also takes time to build such a relationship.
    1.2.1 *Upon approaching a specific franchisor, the prospective franchisee will be honest and forthright in disclosing his or her personal circumstances, talents and skills, personal preferences and available resources.*
    1.2.2 *The prospective franchisee will allocate sufficient time and effort to the task of investigating the opportunity thoroughly by following the guidelines given in the literature mentioned in paragraph 1.1. Should any point remain unclear, they will seek clarification from the franchisor.*
    1.2.3 *Having made a choice in principle, the prospective franchisee will invest the time and funding required to obtain comprehensive professional advice pertaining*

to the viability and suitability of the franchise under consideration.

2 OBLIGATIONS DURING THE IMPLEMENTATION STAGE

Once the franchise agreement has been signed, the franchisee will file it away safely and focus on building his or her business within the franchised network. To this end, the franchisee undertakes to do the following:

2.1 *Embrace the network's identity without reservations. Furthermore, the franchisee will:*
  2.1.1 *Attend initial and ongoing training sessions offered by the franchisor.*
  2.1.2 *Embrace the network's brand, systems and procedures as communicated during training and set out in the operations and procedures manual.*
  2.1.3 *Cooperate fully with the network's field service representatives and other support staff.*
  2.1.4 *Participate enthusiastically in all activities arranged by the franchisor for the benefit of members of the network.*
  2.1.5 *Liaise with fellow-franchisees in a spirit of goodwill and cooperation. If called upon to do so, make him/herself available to serve on the network's marketing committee, franchisee representative committee or similar structure.*

3 GENERAL GUIDELINES

3.1 *The franchisee will channel all available time and resources into initiatives to make the franchise the best business of its kind in the territory.*
3.2 *The franchisee will fulfil all his/her obligations as set out in the franchise agreement.*
3.3 *The franchisee will defend the network's brand and reputation against attack by third parties, uphold its standing at all times and notify the franchisor of serious threats, be they reputation or product related, as they become apparent.*

3.4 *Should disagreements between the franchisee and/or the franchisor including members of the franchise support team or fellow franchisees arise, the franchisee will actively strive towards a resolution that keeps the integrity of the network intact and allows for a win–win outcome. Should no resolution be found, the franchisee will submit him/herself to mediation or arbitration.*

4 INDUSTRY PARTICIPATION

Franchisees recognize that it is in their own best interest to stay informed about developments in the franchise sector, be prepared to actively participate in sector initiatives and generally conduct their businesses in a manner that is likely to foster franchising's reputation.

Service providers (affiliates)

For the purposes of this section, the term service provider includes banks that provide finance to franchised entities, solicitors who undertake franchise-related legal work, and franchise consultants. Although the role of service providers is largely an indirect one, they are in a position to exert strong influence over the major role players and the way they conduct their franchises. As such, service providers must accept some responsibility for the implementation of best practices in franchising. It follows that service providers who wish to be recognized by the burgeoning franchise sector as franchise professionals should adhere to the guidelines set out below.

1 GENERAL

1.1 *All service providers will familiarize themselves fully with the way franchising works. Quality information is available from several sources – see Chapter 7.*
1.2 *All service providers should seek affiliate membership of their national franchise association.*

2 BANKERS

Bankers who wish to be recognized as preferred providers of finance to the franchise sector will not provide franchise finance to members of a franchised network unless this network conducts its franchise in accordance with the national franchise association's Code of Ethics and Business Practices.

3 LEGAL PRACTITIONERS

Solicitors who wish to be recognized as preferred suppliers of legal services to the franchise sector undertake to:

3.1 *Assess requests for the drafting of franchise agreements realistically, keeping in mind that the best franchise agreement will not salvage an inherently weak franchise.*

3.2 *Use their best endeavours to guide prospective franchisors towards compliance with best practices in franchising, especially towards the realization that for a franchised network to prosper, the franchise agreement should be fair and balanced.*

3.3 *Accept that a clear and unmistakable link exists between the franchise agreement and the operations and procedures manual.*

3.4 *Use their influence to steer franchise clients, be they franchisees or franchisors, who are locked into a dispute, towards informal dispute resolution processes, for example the mediation process offered by some national franchise associations.*

4 CONSULTANTS

Consultants who wish to be recognized as preferred suppliers of consultancy services to the franchise sector undertake to:

4.1 *Compile a disclosure document that provides comprehensive information regarding the background, experience and financial standing of the organization, with specific reference* *being made to the franchise expertise of the partners in the firm. A copy of this document will be made available to every prospective client.*

4.2 *Assess requests for the creation of a franchise package realistically, keeping in mind that the best franchise package will not salvage a poorly funded and/or managed franchise organization.*

4.3 *Encourage franchisors to introduce activities within their networks that are designed to enhance franchisee profitability and the franchisor/franchisee relationship, for example by introducing:*

    4.3.1 *Focused training programmes;*

    4.3.2 *Effective dispute resolution mechanisms that are non-confrontational.*

4.4 *Endeavour to guide prospective franchisors towards:*

    4.4.1 *Compliance with best practices in franchising.*

    4.4.2 *Seeking membership of their national franchise association.*

4.5 *Encourage franchisors to commission regular franchisee satisfaction surveys and act on the results in a decisive manner.*

Index